When Rights Embrace Responsibilities

When Rights Embrace Responsibilities

Biocultural Rights and the Conservation of Environment

GIULIA SAJEVA

OXFORD
UNIVERSITY PRESS

OXFORD
UNIVERSITY PRESS

Oxford University Press is a department of the University of Oxford.
It furthers the University's objective of excellence in research, scholarship,
and education by publishing worldwide. Oxford is a registered trademark of
Oxford University Press in the UK and in certain other countries.

Published in India by
Oxford University Press
2/11 Ground Floor, Ansari Road, Daryaganj, New Delhi 110 002, India

© Oxford University Press 2018

First Edition published in 2018

ISBN-13 (print edition): 978-0-19-948515-4
ISBN-10 (print edition): 0-19-948515-1

ISBN-13 (eBook): 978-0-19-909189-8
ISBN-10 (eBook): 0-19-909189-7

Typeset in Adobe Jenson Pro 11/15
by Tranistics Data Technologies, New Delhi 110 044
Printed in India by Replika Press Pvt. Ltd

To the woman without whom I would not be here
but who is not here

Contents

Preface		ix
Acknowledgements		xi
List of Abbreviations		xv
Introduction		xvii
Chapter 1	An Environmental Crisis	1
Chapter 2	Understanding Rights, Human Rights, and Group Rights	21
Chapter 3	Friends and Foes: Rights, the Environment, and People	50
Chapter 4	Of Rights and Responsibilities	76
Chapter 5	Biocultural Rights: Handle with Care	115
Chapter 6	Past, Present, and Future: Beyond Biocultural Rights	142
Bibliography		155
Index		173
About the Author		185

Preface

When I began my studies, I was told that I had to choose with whom to take sides: human rights or conservation of the environment. Even though the environment has been widely recognized to be fundamental for the fulfilment of human rights, conservation practices carry the legacy of a history of human rights violations—particularly when it comes to the rights of indigenous peoples and local communities. At the same time, human rights protection has not always been, nor is, primarily concerned with environmental considerations, to the point of regarding it as an unimportant contingency in some cases.

When I encountered Sanjay Kabir Bavikatte's work on biocultural rights, it immediately caught my attention as an interesting key to work on the combination of care for both human rights and the environment. I then moved beyond the moment of enchantment for biocultural rights and I began to see—and be shown—their problems. But I remained fascinated. Perfection is boring. I hence engaged in a PhD on the analysis of biocultural rights, trying to understand their structure, raison d'être, advantages, and disadvantages, and I found a very thought-provoking and challenging core.

This book is the development of the thesis that I wrote for the PhD programme 'Human Rights: Evolution, Protection and Limits', of the Department of Law at the Università degli Studi di Palermo, Italy.

Edited versions of some of the arguments and parts developed in Chapters 3, 4, and 5 were earlier published as Sajeva (2015;[1] 2017[2]).

---

[1] Reproduced with permission of the Licensor through PLSclear.

[2] Reproduced with permission of Società editrice il Mulino.

Acknowledgements

A cknowledgements and thanks are always one of the hardest parts of a book to write. No one can tell you who you forgot to thank, not even your reviewers. But the forgotten ones will know....

I surely have to thank my supervisors and friends, Bruno Celano and Nicola Gullo of the Università degli Studi di Palermo, for supporting and counselling me during and after my PhD. For actually creating, running, and making the PhD in 'a precious learning experience Human Rights: Evolution, Protection and Limits', I would also like to thank Francesco Viola, Isabel Trujillo, and Aldo Schiavello (Università degli Studi di Palermo). Thank you also to my fellow PhD students of the Aula Dottorandi (in particular the *discipuli Bruni*: Matija Žgur, Giuseppe Rocché, and Enrico La Grassa), without whom writing would have not been so much fun!

I must especially thank Luca Sineo, Renato Chemello, and Maurizio Sajeva (Università degli Studi di Palermo) for helping a non-hard-scientist to understand something about their disciplines.

This book would not have evolved around so many issues, and would not have benefited from on-the-ground experience without the help and friendship of Gino Cocchiaro, Lesle Jansen, and the entire

Natural Justice: Lawyers for Communities and the Environment team— Thank you for welcoming me in Cape Town. I owe a special thanks to Harry Jonas for the constructive challenges offered against my ideas, which helped me to better see the limits of biocultural rights.

For reading my PhD thesis, commenting on it, and posing so many important questions, and for being the friendliest PhD viva examiner one could hope for, thank you, Gary Martin.

My writing has also profited greatly from the comments and suggestions of the many that attended seminars and presentations on the raw versions of the book. I would hence like to thank Ilan Kelman and John Fellows for organizing and engaging in my seminar at University College London; Elisa Morgera and Stephanie Switzer for hosting my presentation at the University of Strathclyde; John Tasioulas for the comments given at the Cambridge Doctoral Workshop on Legal Theory; and Katharine N. Farrell and Konrad Hagedorn (Humboldt-Universität zu Berlin) and David Barkin (Universidad Autonoma Metropolitana) for hosting me for a wonderful and fruitful time at Berlin Workshop in Institutional Analysis of Social-Ecological Systems (WINS), Humboldt-Universität zu Berlin. A further thank you is also due to Anna Grear and Bas Verschuuren for their observations and suggestions.

I am grateful to the two blind reviewers for the comments and suggestions provided on my text, and to Giusi Todaro for helping me go through their comments with a book editor's eye. A sincere thanks goes to the team at Oxford University Press India who so patiently guided me, went through my many mistakes, and tolerated my delays.

A special thanks is for Lisa Schmid, for her intelligent, patient, and attentive support during the revision of my countless drafts (and for being there in my moments of panic). Thank you, Nina Hall, for suggesting such a precious draft editor.

My deepest, warmest, and most deserved 'thank you' is for the man who believed in me, cheered me up, read and re-read my drafts, took care of me during my writing, clarified my ideas, saw my mistakes, and stayed up until late to help me. To the man I am so lucky to have married, *grazie* Marco Brigaglia.

I also owe my thanks to the love and care of my father and brother, Maurizio and Luca Sajeva, and to my beautiful bridesmaids, Adriana Tusa, Laura Di Fede and Lidia Noto, for giving me strength, love, and faith while writing this book.

My last, sincere, and vital thank you goes to Sanjay Kabir Bavikatte for his inspiring and precious work on biocultural rights and for his faith in the stewards of the earth.

Grazie a tutti,
Giulia

Abbreviations

AU	African Union
BCP	Biocultural Community Protocol
CBD	Convention on Biological Diversity
FAO	Food and Agriculture Organization of the United Nations
ICCA	Indigenous Peoples and Local Communities' Conserved Territories and Areas
ICESCR	International Covenant on Economic, Social and Cultural Rights
ICCPR	International Covenant on Civil and Political Rights
ILO	International Labour Organization
IRDNC	Integrated Rural Development and Nature Conservation
ITPGRFA	International Treaty on Plant Genetic Resources for Food and Agriculture
IUCN	International Union for Conservation of Nature
MoEF	Ministry of Environment and Forests
REDD	Reducing Emissions from Deforestation and Forest Degradation
REDD+	Reducing Emissions from Deforestation and Forest Degradation and the role of conservation, sustainable management of forests and enhancement of forest carbon stocks in developing countries

TRRs	Traditional Resource Rights
UDHR	Universal Declaration of Human Right
UN	United Nations
UNDRIP	United Nations Declaration on the Rights of Indigenous Peoples
UNEP	United Nations Environment Programme
UNFCCC	United Nations Framework Convention on Climate Change
UNGA	United Nations General Assembly
UNHCHR	United Nations High Commissioner for Human Rights
WINS	Berlin Workshop in Institutional Analysis of Social-Ecological Systems
WWF	World Wide Fund for Nature

Introduction

Often, the campaigns of indigenous communities are misjudged as the ignorance of 'primitives' unschooled in modern economic realities. But make no mistake. We are not peoples of the past—we are your contemporaries and in some ways may be your guides towards more sustainable futures in the twenty-first century.[1]

In the last 30 years, indigenous peoples have proposed themselves as leaders in the movement for conservation of the environment on the ground that their traditional ethics display humans as custodians of the earth.[2] This book explores the meaning and significance of the concept of biocultural rights,[3] as theorized by Sanjay Kabir Bavikatte in his book *Stewarding the Earth: Rethinking Property*

---

[1] Indigenous peoples' address the United Nations General Assembly Special Session, 22–23 June 1997, delivered by Joji Carino, cited in Gray (1999: 6). This citation marks the closing of Bavikatte (2014).

[2] See, for example, Posey (1999a).

[3] This term is inspired by the term 'biocultural diversity' that was used by Darrell A. Posey to describe the idea of long-term, sustainable, and mutually beneficial relationships between certain communities and peoples and the environment; see Posey (1999b).

and the Emergence of Biocultural Rights. He has recently introduced the term 'biocultural rights' to describe a basket of human rights—group rights in particular—aimed at protecting the stewardship role that certain indigenous peoples and local communities have maintained towards the environment. He argues that biocultural rights are *emerging* from the interpretation of the texts and negotiating documents of multilateral environmental agreements, such as the Convention on Biological Diversity (CBD), and court cases, such as the *Endorois Welfare Council v. Kenya.*[4]

The concept of biocultural rights attempts to suggest strategies for claims inspired by non-mainstream ethics which aim at benefiting peoples, communities, and the environment. The discourse around biocultural rights provides a forum of enquiry concerning new ways to face the current environmental crisis, where indigenous peoples and local communities act as important co-agents in building alternative approaches. Biocultural rights are a proposal for the harmonization of environmental and human rights interests through the shaping of a sui generis basket of human rights, which builds on environmentally sound world views and customary laws that certain indigenous peoples and local communities have maintained. Their ethics and practices, based on the idea of a responsibility towards the environment, enable the combination of the two interests in a way that has, until recently, been underexplored: the recognition of human rights to indigenous peoples and local communities not only to promote their interests and needs but also in order to promote conservation of the environment.

Since their appearance in the international debate, biocultural rights have been welcomed by many scholars and activists and have been challenged by just as many. The three main points of critique received so far are very different from each other: the first concerns

---

[4] Decision of the African Commission on Human and Peoples Rights. Communication 276/2003.

the territory of justice, the second invokes scientific facts, and the third is placed in the realm of international law. The first and most important one, which appeals to justice itself, stresses the potential inequalities and dangers that are lurking behind such an appealing idea and that may potentially hinder the interests of indigenous peoples; the second challenges the very underpinning of biocultural rights, questioning the assumption that indigenous peoples and local communities have a role in the conservation of the environment; and the third proclaims the non-existence of biocultural rights in international law, either as custom or principles, or in treaty law.

This book attempts to steer around these three icebergs, trying not to move too close to any of them. It does not take a stance on what is the current degree of legal recognition of biocultural rights in international, regional, or national law. It rather deals with the possible merits of biocultural rights, the reasons to welcome and support their *coming alive*, as well as with the problems stemming from their very structure.

Biocultural rights entail political implications that cannot be, and are not, ignored. This book's aspiration is to understand the value as well as the threats behind claims for biocultural rights in order to provide a starting point from which it should be easier to decide whether and how to use them in the most appropriate way. It can be seen as an attempt to safely take biocultural rights to the other side of the ocean. Nevertheless, not all books have a happy ending, and the story of biocultural rights reaching the opposite shore has not been written yet. Posterity will judge.

The book is divided into six chapters. The first three are dedicated to the description of the landscape and context of the discourse upon which biocultural rights is built—an indispensable step to understand why dealing with biocultural rights is important. The environmental crisis, the difficulty of human rights theory in accommodating environmental issues, the history of conservation practices in relation to indigenous peoples and local communities—these are all matters which are essential to place biocultural rights in the current legal, environmental, and ethical framework. These three chapters are also dedicated to a reconstruction of the main instruments necessary to fully engage with the analysis of biocultural rights—instruments, such as different environmental ethics theories, and the theory of human rights.

More specifically, Chapter 1 offers an overview of the current environmental crisis and provides an introduction to the different ethical approaches aimed at coping with this crisis. As a first step in a convoluted journey towards the discovery of biocultural rights, the chapter looks for the environmental approaches most suitable to accommodate conservation efforts and, interestingly but not surprisingly, finds them in those theories that come closer to world views of indigenous peoples.

Chapter 2 provides an introduction to the development of the concept of rights, including the birth of human rights and group rights—both of which are useful for understanding the sui generis features of biocultural rights. They might, in fact, appear as a conventional, rather than sui generis, set of group rights if not enough attention is given to the foundations of human rights, the relation between human rights and general interest, and the hardship of balancing human rights and other interests and goals. Chapter 2 also introduces a brief outline of the rights of indigenous peoples and local communities, focusing on their different status in international law. This allows for comparing biocultural rights with other human rights of indigenous peoples and local communities and for elaborating on the different significance biocultural rights have for local communities and for indigenous peoples.

Chapter 3 explores the controversial relationship of interdependence and conflict between environmental concerns and the protection of human rights. It offers insights on the necessity—and the opportunity—of new ideas such as biocultural rights. This can only be made clear if we bring forward, on the one hand, the damages environmental conservation can cause to the human rights of indigenous peoples and local communities, and, on the other hand, the inadequacy of the human rights rhetoric in incorporating environmental challenges. Chapter 3 introduces attempts to combine these two interests based on the stewardship relationship of indigenous peoples and local communities towards the environment, while keeping distance from the dangers of the myth of the noble savage.

Building on the notions and instruments to which the first three chapters are devoted, the last three analyse the conceptual structure of biocultural rights and explore the opportunities and risks coming with them. Chapter 4 examines the concept of biocultural rights, from a legal theory perspective. After paying tribute to Bavikatte's theory, it explores the definition of biocultural rights, their foundations, their rights and duty holders, the conditions of stewardship, and the rights necessary to preserve such a stewardship role. Starting from the claim that the foundations of biocultural rights are two concurring ones, exploring Darrell Posey's concept of traditional resources rights—shedding light on their roots and innovative features—and dismissing the noble savage myth, biocultural rights are analysed to fully understand what biocultural rights are and what they are not. The foundations of biocultural rights are then explored in detail, focusing on the problems arising from the fact that biocultural rights, besides conferring rights to their holders, also seem to confer a set of duties.

Chapter 5 explores the difficult and challenging questions that arise from the sui generis nature of biocultural rights: they carry certain characteristics that are typical of the human rights discourse as well as others that are difficult to fit into its categories. A reflection is provided on the potential positive and negative implications biocultural rights entail from political and practical points of view, stressing the different status of indigenous peoples and local communities in international law, and pointing out how this influences the potential dangers and advantages of biocultural rights. In order to explore how biocultural rights could be valuable, albeit when handled with care, Chapter 5 provides an analysis of the case of the Khwe indigenous peoples of Bwabwata National Park, investigating their struggles and claims through the lens of biocultural rights.

Finally, Chapter 6 draws some conclusions on human rights in the Anthropocene and elaborates on the future of biocultural rights, suggesting developments that move beyond indigenous peoples as potential holders of biocultural rights and tries to overcome their potentially unfair implications.

1   An Environmental Crisis

Facing Responsibilities

> Homo sapiens has produced all the most fascinating and horrible, useful
> and superfluous, creative and devastating things it could have ever done
>
> —Chelazzi 2013: 179; author's translation

When you first attempt to write a chapter about the environmental crisis[1] you wonder what, really, you can add to the current discussion, especially if you are neither a conservation scientist, an ecologist, nor a hard scientist at all. The topic

---

[1] The term 'environmental crisis' has been used since the 1970s by scientists to refer to a growing number of environmental disasters; see Park (2001: 4). Today, the environmental crisis comprises problems such as climate change, depletion of the ozone layer, acid rain, destruction of tropical forests

seems to have been twisted and turned over and over again in far too many books and articles. The current environmental crisis is something every layperson has heard about; it is a mantra we hear every day on the news, on social networks, even in the novels we read. There are also people who caution us against exaggerations, not really because human beings are not injuring the earth, but mostly to avoid panicking (Lombrog 1998: 5)[2]—panic, as is commonly known, does not lead to wise and informed decisions, and in conservation science, the variables and issues to be considered are far too many and complex to be decided upon in haste. This point is emphasized because the rights of indigenous peoples and local communities are some of the issues that are far too often put on hold in a hurry (if not to give space to other, less noble, interests).

Accordingly, let us stop for a second and try to look at the bigger picture, bigger than the earth: the earth, along its history and human beings within it. Human beings are not the only species which have modified ecosystems: '[a]ll forms of life modify their context' (White 1967: 1203). And many non-human species pollute and even lead others to extinction, not only invasive species introduced by humans.[3] History is characterized by species succession: some have evolved into others, others have gone extinct, and a few have remained still. Some have gone extinct because of habitat, climatic, or even extra-terrestrial[4] changes, and others because of other species: they were hunted to extinction, their nutriment was exhausted or territory occupied. And

---

(Park 2001: 5–9), as well the loss of biodiversity, air and water pollution, and the unsustainable use of natural resources.

[2] See also the back cover of the book by D.N. Adams (1979), which says, 'Do Not Panic!' in very large letters.

[3] This chapter refers mostly to the loss of biodiversity, using it as a proxy for a more heterogeneous term, global environmental crisis.

[4] This does not mean the arrival of extra-terrestrial life on earth, but the impact of meteorites.

many, too many, have gone extinct because of human beings. Long before the advent of technology, including in prehistoric times, human beings caused the extinction of many species, even species which would have been useful for human development.[5]

Is there something that gives us—as a species—a capacity for destruction, which is superior to that of other species? Or is it just our ability to understand the consequences of our actions that makes us aware of our ecological footprint, and that makes us feel guilty about what we do? This chapter argues for the first. First of all, we are not plants. But we are not the only non-plant. We are also primates and we share complex social behaviours with other primates, we use instruments, and transmit some forms of knowledge across generations (Chelazzi 2013: 36). Homo sapiens is only 150–200,000 years old,[6] which is very young compared to other species, including the extinct species of Homo. Humans of the lower and medium Pleistocene epoch were part of the small group of super predators who did not particularly change the surrounding ecosystems. Across the centuries, human culture progressively increased, showing an incredible ecological plasticity (Chelazzi 2013: 71), together with the ambition to explore new worlds for the sake of curiosity rather than simple hunger.

Homo sapiens spread around the world from southern Africa to South America, reaching places no other hominid had reached before, benefiting from its ability to take very different ecological roles: hunters, veldt product and beach gatherers, fishers, scavengers, frugivores, and herbivores (Chelazzi 2013: 60). Being omnivores and all-rounders, we are less affected by the decline of the population of a single prey species: we have many others to turn to. Moreover, we are

---

[5] For example, large mammals that could have been domesticated; see Diamond (1997).

[6] The average lifespan of a species is between 1 and 10 million years, according to Lombrog (1998: 251).

particularly aggressive hunters: no other animal in the wild hunts for sport (let us ignore the neighbour's cat), though we are not the only ones to hunt for non-subsistence reasons. Lions, for example, kill the cubs of hyenas to prevent future competition and kill other lions' offspring to mate with lionesses. But we are the only animals to hunt to make clothes and utensils or to fulfil symbolic needs (rites of passage, sacrifices, and so on).

We create tools to obtain other tools that allow us to get very different types of food and, most importantly, we are able to adapt to very different ecosystems. We were selected based on biocultural characteristics that make us able to solve unforeseen problems in very different conditions (Chelazzi 2013: 61). We have a brain that allows us to develop abstract thoughts and solve high-level problems, and coordinate groups through language and writing (Chelazzi 2013: 61, 64). Our mental abilities lead us to desire things that go beyond the simple satisfaction of primary instincts (Chelazzi 2013: 87), and push us to look for new realities, new tools, new foods, new places. Our brain has also allowed us to domesticate other species—animals and plants—which we have brought with us, introducing cats, dogs, and pigs in ecosystems defenceless against them. The division of labour might also have promoted the increase in human population, which in turn stimulates the production of new forms of cooperation and technology.

These abilities and desires and our increasing population led scholars to accuse us of 'ecocide' through overkill during our expansion throughout the world at the end of the Pleistocene (Martin 1996; Wilson 2001: 536–61), which was shortly before entering the current geological time, the Holocene, about 12,000 years ago. Our arrival as skilled hunters in new areas and the discovery of new weapons was taken as the driver of the extinction of about 180 species of megafauna (animals weighing more than 44 kilograms) (Chelazzi 2013: 106, 113), consequently damaging the surrounding vegetation and ecosystems at large. However, many scholars have warned against holding the few Homo sapiens living at that time entirely responsible, and have suggested that it seems more likely that the damage to ecosystems was the result of a combination of factors where humans dealt the final blow to species that had reached the end of their cycle.[7] Moreover, where humans destructed they also sometimes created, contributing to the increase of a certain biodiversity[8]—a niche group of domesticated species—among which may be included selected varieties of olives, grapes, goats, and cows (Chelazzi 2013: 257).

Regardless whether we were fully responsible for Pleistocene extinction, it is sure that 'human hunters help no species' (Wilson 2001: 558) and 'with the end of moderate-impact cultivation practices and with the agricultural intensification associated with the Industrial Revolution—mechanization, use of fertilizers and pesticides and exaggerated monocultures—the situation definitely plunged' (Chelazzi 2013: 259). It plunged so far that we are talking about the sixth mass extinction (Barnosky et al. 2001; Ceballos et al., 2015)—characterized by the disappearance, in a definite lapse of time, of entire genera and classes (Pievani 2002: 321). The other Big Five mass extinctions (Barnosky et al. 2001; Pievani 2002: 317) occurred between 443 and 65 million years ago and were consisted in extinctions ranging from 75 to 96 per cent of species (Chelazzi 2013: 118). Today, rates of extinction estimated by experts diverge very widely (Pearce 2015)—from 1 per cent to 30 per cent of global biodiversity loss per decade. Such variation might disorientate the conservation scientist, as well

---

[7] See the debate between Paul Martin and Louis Seymour Bazett Leakey in Chelazzi (2013: 125–36).

[8] According to Article 2 of the CBD, biodiversity is the term used to describe the 'variability among living organisms from all sources including, inter alia, terrestrial, marine, and other aquatic ecosystems and the ecological complexes of which they are a part; this includes diversity within species and of ecosystems.'

as the environmental philosopher. It is due to the fact that only 1,200 extinctions have been recorded in the last 400 years, while all other figures are estimates, calculated using different methods and models (Pearce 2015; Stork 2010). However, although not precise, these figures point in one direction,[9] and the current extinction is characterized by a point of important originality: it is generated mostly, or only, by one single species, Homo sapiens (Pievani 2002: 329).

In order to describe the current situation, in 2000, Paul Crutzen, winner of the Nobel Prize, suggested that the earth had exited the Holocene and entered a new geological epoch: the Anthropocene (Hamilton, Bonneuil, and Gemenne 2015: 1). It can be described as an epoch characterized by a radical change in the relationship between humans and the environment, where human force is able to influence nature in unprecedentedly destructive ways (Boyd 2012: 10). As a geological epoch, the Anthropocene has not yet been validated by the International Commission on Stratigraphy, but it is widely used by scientists and the media 'to designate the period of Earth's history during which humans have a decisive influence on the state, dynamics and future of the Earth system' (Subcommission on Quaternary Stratigraphy 2016; Zalasiewicz, Waters, and Head 2017).

Regardless of whether it can be considered a geological epoch, the Anthropocene can be used as a metaphor to draw attention to the impact human beings have on the earth. Today, ecosystems and their diversity are under anthropogenic threat more than ever, due to technologies which were unthought of in the Pleistocene, and due to the growth of the human population to more than a thousand times its size at that time. Today's anthropogenic threats range from habitat destruction, habitat fragmentation and degradation, climate change,

[9] The International Union for Conservation of Nature and Natural Resources (IUCN) Red List designates 7,781 species as endangered, and 5,210 as critically endangered (as on 24 February 2017).

overexploitation, and introduction of invasive species, to the circulation of exotic diseases. We have the power to damage the earth's biodiversity as no other species has had before, thanks to the combination of those abilities and characteristics that differentiate us from other species. These features, however, also make us able to understand the consequences of our actions. We are more harmful than a hunting lion and we are also able to witness and foresee the damage we produce— damage which harms biodiversity and ourselves. We destroy our own habitat and many species whose sight gives us pleasure, whose meat and fibre give us nutrients, and whose bioactive components give us (or could, in the future, give us) medicines.

One last, but really not least, point must be underlined before moving to very different grounds of discussion. After each of the Big Five mass extinctions, life on earth came back, as diverse and prosperous as before. Not after a few years of course, but it eventually did. Hence, even if we generate the sixth mass extinction, life on earth will not be lost. It will come back without us—over and over until the Sun swallows the earth, together with Mercury, Venus, and Mars in a few hundreds of millions of years (Reeves et al. 1996: 83). Does that give us hope or moderate our reasons for fear? It probably does not. We remain, rightly, afraid and guilty of the consequences of our actions, regardless of the fact that they are very trivial vis-à-vis the history of the universe.

The Human, the Living, the Cosmos: Searching for Environmental Ethics

A Matter of Value

When we talk about the current environmental crisis, we do not have in mind only birds and rivers, elephants and trees. We directly link such a crisis to a human crisis, a crisis that negatively affects human beings all over the world (Millennium Ecosystem Assessment 2005: 2; Sheehan and Wilson 2015). The conservation of the environment is in fact a prerequisite for the well-being, and the very survival, of humankind. Degraded ecosystems cannot provide ecological services— food, water, building material, clean air—which are essential to fulfil human needs and avoid human suffering. This idea brings us to the widely discussed problem of the value of the environment in relation to human beings, which is one of the most debated issue in the field of environmental ethics and is the distinctive feature of anthropocentric and non-anthropocentric ethics.

Environmental ethics is the field of ethics particularly concerned with the relationship between humans and the environment. Officially born about 40 years ago, it is a somewhat new field (although humans have always reasoned about their behaviour in their habitats), which finds itself confronted by an urgent need to change something in the relationship between humans and the environment. The entry into the Anthropocene, and the increased footprint of humankind on earth, has fuelled the need to create an appropriate environmental ethic—or ethics[10]—to monitor and orientate human activities, may they be social, political, or scientific. What the famous environmental philosopher Hans Jonas (1984) refers to as the 'traditional ethic' is not suitable anymore to guide human behaviour, because it is not shaped around the understanding of the threat humankind has increasingly become to nature. Jonas (1984) argues that a shift towards an ethic of responsibility is indispensable, an ethic that understands nature as something given in custody to humankind, something towards which we must assume the role of a custodian. Although it is often

---

[10] For the purposes of this book, there is no need to enter the complex discussion about moral pluralism and monism in the realm of environmental ethics. It is, however, an interesting ongoing debate, which questions the existence, or lack, of one set of overarching principles which ought to govern all ethical activities; see Stone (1998), and for the opposing position, see Callicott (1990).

inadequate to generalize, he predominantly refers to Western[11] ethics (Routley and Routley 1980: 123), Western impact on the planet, and Western approaches towards the environment.

Western environmental ethics can be described as being divided into two main streams, both striving to answer the same question: how do we understand what ought to be recognized value and why? Anthropocentric and non-anthropocentric ethics provide different answers to the what, but, more importantly, to the why. The most intuitive means of attributing value to something is to understand whether something is useful, or has utility. In general, something is considered valuable if it has a utility for human beings,[12] either directly or indirectly (for example, an edible plant or a substance useful to make edible plants grow faster). This kind of value is referred to as non-intrinsic, instrumental value: something has non-intrinsic value if it is a means to some other end, if its value is derivative because it does not lie in the thing itself but in something else for which it is relevant. In order to understand whether something has non-intrinsic value, we need to find something that comes before it in a chain of values, and which justifies the value to be attributed. But this chain cannot be infinite. There must be something, in the end, that is considered to have intrinsic value, which is 'the value that that thing has "in itself", or "for its own sake", or "as such", or "in its own right"' (Zimmerman 2015: 1). Such intrinsic value is non-instrumental, it cannot be deduced by the utility for something or someone else: 'an object has intrinsic value if it is an end in itself' (O'Neill 1992).[13]

---

[11] The term Western is, indeed, an oversimplification, which builds on a common but implicit understanding of the concept. It is used here to describe the legal, economic, and cultural system prevailing in Europe, North America, Australia, and New Zealand (as well as, increasingly, in the Republic of South Africa).

[12] The Routleys refer to this as conventional utility; see Benson (2000).

[13] Though this is the most common understanding of the concept of intrinsic value, it is necessary to underline that it is an ambiguous term, which

Environmental ethics are grounded on different perceptions of whether the environment or some of its elements have non-instrumental value. The common division between anthropocentric and non-anthropocentric ethics corresponds to that between shallow and deep ecology,[14] terms coined by Arne Naess, based on sharp opposition between instrumental and non-instrumental value. Naess attributes a strong non-instrumental position concerning the value of the environment to the deep ecology concept: 'the wellbeing and flourishing of human and non-human life on Earth have value in themselves', regardless of 'the usefulness of the non-human world for human purposes' (Naess 2003: 264). In contrast, shallow ethical views support a vision according to which the environment has value only insofar as it is relevant for human well-being. From these two opposing positions, many intermediate theories have been formulated.

Anthropocentric Approaches

Anthropocentric approaches to conservation of the environment are considered to be most efficient for convincing people to respect the

---

can also be defined in a second and third sense: the second referring solely to the non-relational properties of an object, and the third referring to an objective value, independent of any value-attributing subject. For the purposes of this book, intrinsic value will be considered only in the first sense, clarifying the fact that being attributed intrinsic value in the first sense does not imply attribution of intrinsic value in the second and third senses. For example, wilderness can be considered to have intrinsic value in the first sense. However, it does not have intrinsic value in the second sense, because the concept of wilderness implies the idea of (a lack of) contact with human beings, which is a relational consideration (second sense of the term).

[14] Ecology is the study of a habitat and of the interactions between its biological and non-living elements. In the sense used in environmental ethics studies, ecology refers to the study of human habitat and its interactions with all non-human elements.

environment. 'It is in your interest to respect the environment' or 'if you damage the environment you damage humankind/yourself' are surely the most commonly diffused arguments in favour of promoting respect and condemning disrespect towards the environment. In these arguments, the environment does not figure as a holder of value per se, but as the holder of value for the sake of humankind, towards which we hold responsibilities. These arguments are not grounded in the existence of a set of responsibilities towards the environment, but rather in our responsibilities towards other human beings (including ourselves).

Anthropocentric ethics are the direct successors of Western ethics, as they are a reinterpretation of the same ethical grounds (Passmore 1974: 186–7, cited in DesJardins 2013: 102). They build on the understanding of the duty to respect other human beings and, by extending the needs of human beings to those concerning the environment, they include duties to conserve it. Such duties, however, are not towards the environment, they simply *regard* the environment. They are duties towards humankind and are 'a matter of prudence' (DesJardins 2013: 98).

Anthropocentric views are strongly criticized precisely for their focus on human interests. Such a focus can justify, as many authors claim, the use of the environment 'merely as a storehouse of raw materials to be extracted and used for products serving human preferences' (Norton 1984: 135). However, according to some authors, anthropocentric views can push the borders of environmental protection beyond the mere conservation of natural resources instrumentally valuable to humans. For example, the survival of unspoiled natural environments contributes to human well-being (Benson 2000: 85), so the concern for environmental protection may be extended to assets that are not to be materially used by humans, but which are to be objects of wonder, knowledge, or piety.[15] Aesthetic considerations can play a role in supporting the expansion of duties to protect the environment beyond

---

[15] For an analysis of different positions to extend the borders of environmental protection, see Benson (2000: chapter 4).

what could directly be harmed, or be used, by human beings and allow the incorporation of elements that foster human well-being at a higher level. Science, the sake of knowledge, awe, and wonder, the capacity to feel piety, and simply being glad when looking at natural elements are abilities that can lead humans to enter into a relationship with the environment without consumption and exploitation, but simply through a conservation-oriented contemplation. Such human abilities are components of human well-being; hence, their exercise benefits humans while at the same time, they promote environmental protection (Benson 2000: 79, 82).

Accordingly, anthropocentric ethics, if perceived in a weak sense, can provide 'a framework for developing strong reasons for protecting nature' (Norton 1984: 135). Norton claims that if human interests—cleared from superficial whims and preferences—and carefully weighted desires and needs are sewed together using a non-individualistic approach, they can provide the ground for a solid environmental ethic. Norton's position originates from the ideal of human harmony with nature and the assumption that human consciousness has to be perpetuated, and pushes the borders of the anthropocentric environmental ethic, enlarging the extent of human interests by including, in a non-individualistic turn, the interests of future generations. This approach remains anthropocentric but provides reasons for restrictions on the use of natural resources that would not occur if only present generations were considered. His focus on non-individualistic approaches goes in fact beyond a first layer of non-harm to other individuals, and encompasses a second layer, which requires indefinite conservation of natural resources for the sake of future generations.

Future generations have fully entered the realm of environmental ethics since the famous Brundtland Report, *Our Common Future*, issued in 1987 by the United Nations (UN) World Commission on Environment and Development. The report defines the concept of sustainable development as 'development that meets the needs of the present without compromising the ability of future generations to meet their own needs' (World Commission on Environment and Development 1987: Paragraph I.3.27). What the Brundtland Report suggests is that present generations have the responsibility to conserve the world's natural resources for the sake of future ones. It is a valuable strategy to promote the recognition of duties concerning the environment, which has in fact influenced, and is still influencing, political and economic decisions.

Nevertheless, many environmental ethics philosophers have raised arguments against the idea of responsibilities towards future generations, mainly on two grounds (DesJardins 2013: 78). First, according to the argument based on ignorance, we do not know who the future generations will be and what they will want. Second, following the argument based on disappearing beneficiaries, whatever we do will change those that will be born and those that will not, hence it makes no sense to talk about a future generation. These arguments have been defeated in various ways. We can claim, for instance, that we can be reasonably sure that future generations will have the same (or at least very similar) genetic characters that we have and will, hence, have the same needs that Homo sapiens has had so far (clean air and water, sunlight, plants and animals for food, and so on). We may also maintain that we hold a responsibility to create the best conditions possible for the lives of whoever will come to life in the future, because they are holders of certain fundamental rights (the rights-based approach), because by doing so we minimize total suffering (the utilitarian approach) or because we care for future generations (in the way parents care for their children) (DesJardins 2013: 81–8).

Notions of aesthetic value, the value of knowledge, and future generations extend the borders of environmental protection but remain focused on what is, or will be, thought to be of some value to humans (Benson 2000: 86). Humans remain the loci of value attribution. It surely is a valuable political strategy: policymakers are likely to give little attention to intrinsic value considerations, while they are more likely to consider human-oriented reasons (Norton 1989). But what happens in the absence of the humans? What happens if there remains only one person on earth? Richard Sylvan (Routley) (1973) famously introduces the problem, by imagining a last person remaining on earth who wishes to destroy all ecosystems and natural resources just before her death and the consequent extinction of human species.[16] According to anthropocentric approaches, such an unfortunate and enraged last person has no obligation to restrain herself from destroying whatever she feels like destroying because nothing is needed or will be needed by humans. Routley starts from the presupposition that such destructive actions would be wrong, even if not wrong towards any human beings, and hence suggests that anthropocentrism cannot provide the basis for an adequate environmental ethic. Unless the environment is valued in itself and not seen as only existing for the sake of humans, environmental problems will not be solved (Routley and Routley 1980).

Non-Anthropocentric Approaches

Starting from Aristotle, Aquinas, and Kant and even until the most recent ethicists, the Western tradition hardly ever recognizes the moral standing of entities other than human beings (DesJardins 2013: 100). The environmental challenges we began facing in the last century have, however, inspired many philosophers to answer the call for new environmental ethics, who have built their theories by extending moral considerations to other entities, sometimes to animals retaining certain characteristics, and at other times to all living things, entire species, non-living natural entities, and the earth. To have moral standing means to be a source of moral claim, an entity

---

[16] For a fascinating science-fiction novel on an imaginary last man on earth, see Shiel (1901).

that must be considered in moral deliberations even if it is not linked to the interests, needs, or desires of human beings. We can distinguish three different streams concerning the recognition of moral standing of the environment. The first stream welcomes authors with different views about which animals should be recognized holders of rights. The recognition of moral standing depends on the identification of one or a set of characteristics that a being possesses (being human could also be considered the relevant characteristic, bringing us back to anthropocentric worldviews). Self-consciousness—awareness of one's self, perception of past and future, and sentience—the ability of feeling pain and pleasure, or simply being a living being are among the characteristics most often chosen as necessary and sufficient for having moral standing. A second stream, biocentric ethics, enlarges the realm of moral consideration to all living beings, with being alive becoming the relevant characteristic. A third stream of theories also attributes moral standing to living communities, species, or the earth itself. These differences may only seem superficial, as species and eco-systems are aggregations of the individuals composing them, but as we will see from what follows, in terms of environmental conservation, the differences are relevant.

Animal Rights and Interests

Within the first stream, we may position Joel Feinberg, who bases the recognition of rights to (certain) animals on their conative life, that is, on their ability to have consciousness, desires, and goals. Clearly not all animals (or plants) can be said to have such capacities. Hence, Feinberg argues that only certain higher animals can be granted rights. Such animals have interests that can be promoted or harmed by human actions. Consequently, he argues, adopting an interest theory of rights[17] approach, they hold rights against human beings. The link

---

[17] See Chapter 2 in this book.

between rights-holding and conative capacities only incorporates individual animals and leaves out species and entire ecosystems since they cannot have conative capacities. Along the same lines, Tom Regan (2012) calls for the recognition of the intrinsic value of animals and for the consequent recognition of their rights. All those animals—mostly mammals—that can be 'subjects-of-a-life', which means that they have something similar to beliefs, desires, expectations, and emotional lives, possess value equal to human beings and as such must be treated with equal respect (Regan 1985). Taking a rights-based approach, he argues that no single animal should be harmed—not even on utilitarian considerations. The aggregation of pain or pleasure is not relevant, neither are species and ecosystems. The latter are relevant only insofar as they are composed of individual animals and are important for the fulfilment of their rights (Regan 1985).

Adopting a utilitarian stance, Peter Singer (1975: 7–8) enlarges the focus to lower animals. He finds the source of moral standing in a characteristic that almost all animals have: sentience, that is, the capacity of suffering and enjoyment. This hedonistic approach leads Singer to call for the recognition of equal consideration to all humans and animals. Sentience is the necessary and sufficient requirement to have interests and, consequently, stones, species, or ecosystems cannot have interests and be considered to have moral standing. The overall objective of his ethical approach is not the recognition of rights, but rather the minimization of total suffering, expanding the utilitarian calculus to include animals' pleasure and suffering.

As suggested above, arguing for an individual animal's respect or rights and arguing for species and ecosystems protection differs strongly in terms of environmental consequences. Individualistic environmental ethics cannot properly support environmental conservation movements. Regan, as well as Singer and other promoters of individualistic ethics are more concerned with ending the use of animals for food, research, clothing, and entertainment rather than with the protection of endangered species and whole ecosystems (Regan 1985, 2012). Managing and protecting a species or a habitat, instead, involves recognizing the unequal moral standing of different animals, depending on the species (endangered or abundant) or variety (local or invasive) they are part of. It may also require suppressing invasive species, hunting populations growing beyond maximum carrying capacity, breeding endangered species in captivity, or displacing them (Varner 1995). Because of their willingness to sacrifice individual animals for the 'integrity, stability, and beauty of the biotic community' (Leopold 1949: 242) conservationists are sometimes accused of environmental fascism (Regan 2012). Alongside granting individual animals so much value, individualistic ethics usually advocate giving too little value to other assets. Environmental conservation implies that plants, invertebrate, and fungi are fundamental elements of ecosystems that need to be protected. However, they most often do not qualify as right holders or subjects worthy of moral standing. Besides obvious reasons of credibility (it is easier to defend the claim that elephants have rights than to claim that a fungus does), this approach seems to derive from a never-abandoned anthropocentric approach: those animals (not plants) that qualify for moral standing are precisely those that have characteristics that make them closer to humans than other organisms—such as pain and pleasure, interests, and being subjects-of-a-life. Hence, 'paradigms of holders of moral value are [and remain] human beings' (DesJardins 2013: 118).

Biocentric Ethics

Biocentric theories seem to overcome this concern by recognizing the moral standing of all living beings. One of the first biocentric theories, developed by Paul W. Taylor (1986), regards all animal and plant species as members of the same earth's community of life, a community where members depend on each other and on the overall natural system, and where no hierarchies are acceptable (Taylor 1986: 79–80). Taylor recognizes inherent worth, non-instrumental value, in all living beings for their capacity to—consciously or unconsciously—promote their well-being. Humans are called upon to show an attitude of respect and non-interference towards each of such entities, not only human entities. Notwithstanding his claim for equality, human beings preserve a differentiated role, remaining distinct from nature: they are the ones that have a duty of respect and non-interference (for example, they are the ones called to become vegetarians, other carnivores are not). As most biocentric ethicists do, Taylor maintains an individualistic approach, so species and ecosystems do not fall within his realm of consideration (DesJardins 2013: 143, 151). Similarly, rivers and mountains, landscapes and air are not biological beings and hence are not intrinsically considered worthy of respect. Even though their protection could be promoted for the sake of living beings, biocentric ethics are not sufficient to adequately protect the environment precisely because of their focus on individuals, who cannot be sacrificed even if conservation considerations require them to.

Ecocentric Ethics

In order to accommodate conservation considerations, environmental ethics have to go one step further, towards ecocentric ethics. Ecocentric ethics are holistic, as they place ecological communities at the centre of moral concern and rely deeply on the science of ecology to frame their ethical principles (DesJardins 2013: 152, 163). Ecological communities comprehend living and non-living entities as being part of an interconnected whole. Not all entities are considered worthy of moral standing in their individuality, but rather as elements of the ecosystems whose destiny depends on the interest of the whole. Hence, typical conservation science activities, such as the eradication of invasive species, are acceptable or even promoted, because they aim at the conservation of the 'integrity, stability and beauty of the biotic community' (Leopold 1949: 262). This quote earned Aldo Leopold the accusation of being an environmental fascist (as mentioned earlier). Leopold is one of the principal proponents of holistic ethics (DesJardins 2013: 179), which regards the entire earth, and its ecosystems, as an all-encompassing biotic community possessing a certain degree of life in itself (Leopold 1979). In the essay, 'The Land Ethic', Leopold (1949) extends the borders of moral consideration to all animals, plants, soil, water, and air, but does not cease to regard them as resources, which can be used and managed for and by humans as long as the biotic community and its members are treated with respect. Humans do not have a privileged position; they are members of the earth's community, just like all other natural elements.

Leopold's theory has been criticized for many reasons, and the strongest one relies on the lack of distinction between the 'is' and the 'ought', the naturalist fallacy (DesJardins 2013: 186–94). It is argued that he derives his normative conclusions on the obligation to preserve the integrity, stability, and beauty of ecosystems from his ample reliance on ecology—which is a descriptive science. He does not provide reasons for the recognition of value to the earth's community, he simply states that all natural elements are members of the land community and, since the stability of the latter depends on its integrity, 'they are all entitled to continuance' (Leopold 1949: 247). One possible reply is that this critique could also be directed at other ethical theories, such as those that recognize intrinsic moral value—and a duty of respect— of individual animals because they are sentient beings, or even of humans. The recognition of moral standing of animals, according to Regan, for example, is derived from their conative capacities, which is a description of their natural features.

In order not to regard Regan as succumbing to the naturalist fallacy as well, we presuppose the existence of a norm that prescribes that *those beings that have conative capacities are owed respect*. The same happens with human beings: when we argue that the protection of the environment should be pursued because it is a human interest, we presuppose the normative sentence, 'human interests should be pursued'. Now, one could ask, why has Leopold's argument given rise to such a critique, while no such critiques are directed towards human dignity or animal rights theories? The answer can be inferred from Leopold's writings. The reason seems to lie in current (Western) human psychology, which does not allow us to presuppose, or to take for granted—as we do in other cases—the normative sentence: 'the integrity, stability and beauty of the Earth is to be protected'. Leopold (1949) hopes that through the study and understanding of ecology there can be a change in human psychology, such that we come to love and admire the earth.

This change in human psychology is not something that is achieved easily or quickly. It requires raising awareness about the current environmental crisis, (re-)gaining contact with the natural world, and reframing our relationship with it. Interestingly, it seems that many indigenous peoples and local communities do not need to undertake a psychological turn, as their ethical underpinnings already comprehend different forms of respect and reverence for the earth. This book does not expect to answer the call for the creation of a new ethic. It wants to suggest that there are different traditional ethics (Jonas 1979) that may help humankind in finding new solutions and methods, becoming inspired by those indigenous peoples and local communities, our contemporaries, whose ethics and legal traditions place humankind in the role of a custodian of nature[18] and 'who have become effective leaders in the environment and human rights movement' (Posey 1999a: 15). The idea of biocultural rights, albeit with complications, builds on this custodianship as a possible alternative path to combine conservation of the environment with human rights rhetoric and law.

[18]   According to Callicott (1997: 69), 'The revival and deliberate construction of environmental ethics from the raw materials of indigenous, traditional, and contemporary cognitive cultures represents an important and essential first step in the future movement of human material cultures toward a more symbiotic relationship, however incomplete and imperfect, with the natural environment.'

2 Understanding Rights, Human Rights, and Group Rights

Human Rights from Scratch

What Are Rights?

Biocultural rights have been defined as the basket of human rights of indigenous peoples and local communities required to preserve their role as stewards of the environment. In order to fully understand their significance, it is particularly important to move a step behind and understand the specific characteristics of human rights. In fact, biocultural rights appear as sui generis human rights: so sui generis that one could doubt whether they can really be considered human rights.[1] Of course, human rights do appear in the

---

[1] See Chapter 5 in this book.

discussion about conservation of the environment, but usually in the context of claims for the protection of human interests concerning the environment, such as the right to live in a healthy ecosystem, the right to water, the right to food, the right to clean air, the right to access non-degraded ecosystems, or the rights of future generations to live in a world where natural resources have not been depleted. In the discussion about biocultural rights, instead, human rights serve both classic human interests, in particular, a set of interests of indigenous peoples and local communities, but also a wider environmental one— conservation of the environment. In the chapters that follow, we will see how this anomaly in the context of the current theory of human rights is both problematic and valuably innovative.

In order to analyse the content and implications of a new concept such as biocultural rights, as a special type of rights in the human rights discourse, we first need to convey on and lay out an understanding of *rights* themselves,[2] of their structure, and of their constitutive elements. When adopting an 'interest theory of rights' approach,[3] to say that X has a right means considering a certain interest of X so important as to justify the imposition of a duty on someone else with respect

[2] Most basically, 'right' is a noun, which in the English language has a direct positive connotation, because it overlaps with the adjective used to qualify something as 'correct'. Such an overlap is not casual, but it should not mislead us in thinking that the correspondence is absolute. See, for example, Waldron (1993), which interestingly poses (and positively answers) the question about whether there can be a moral right to do something morally wrong.

[3] In the attempt to answer to the broad question of the justification of rights, two main theories have been developed: the 'will' theory and the 'interest theory'. The underpinning of the will theory of rights is the importance of individual choices, so that a legal right is 'a legally respected choice', see Hart (1982: 189). On the opposite side, the interest theory is based on the importance attributed to the interests of the right holder.

to X's interest.[4] Based on this definition, we can distinguish the following conceptual components of the notion of a right: foundation, right holder, claimant, duty bearer, and content. The interest of X, considered sufficiently important to justify imposing a duty on someone else, is the foundation of the right, its raison d'être. X—a person, a group of people, a minority, the whole human population, future generations, and, according to some scholars, animals, plants, or even the planet[5]—is the right holder. The claimant, instead, is the subject empowered to require the enforcement or the waiver of a right, and it usually overlaps with the right holder (though in certain cases—for example, when the right holder is a child—a different subject may be entitled to this position). The duty bearer is the entity—person, group

---

[4] 'X has a right' when '..., other things being equal, an aspect of X's well-being (his interest) is a sufficient reason for holding some other person(s) to be under a duty', see Raz (1988: 166). See also MacCormick (1976: 305), according to whom, 'having rights is having one's interest protected in certain ways by the imposition of (legal or moral) normative constraints on the acts and activities of other people with respect to the object of one's interest'. Normative constraints may consist of the duty to do or not do something, the lack of right to forbid something to the right holder, the liability to the right holder's power to change a legal position, or the disability to use power against the right holder, or a combination of these duties. This description builds on the framework of legal relations and correlations proposed by Wesley N. Hohfeld. Hohfeld (1919) drew a framework of the legal concepts that he saw implied in the broader and ambiguous concept of 'rights', a term that he thought too often used inappropriately and confusedly in legal discourses. He distilled a set of four legal positions that he saw as composing the concept of a right, which are logically, and necessarily, correlated to four other legal positions (claim–duty/liberty–no claim/power–liability/immunity–disability).

[5] See the subsection titled, 'Non-anthropocentric Ethics' in Chapter 1 of this book.

of people, state, corporation—which holds an obligation with respect to the fulfilment of X's interest. And finally, the content of the right is the set of actions that the duty bearer shall or shall not perform, and/or of a good she/he should provide.

Certain rights are considered to have a particular status, to be special and somehow more powerful than others. This is the status commonly granted to 'human rights' or 'fundamental rights', of which biocultural rights are a sui generis type. The literature on human rights is wide and heterogeneous, as there still seems to be little agreement—as the debate about biocultural rights exemplifies—on their definition, content and, in some cases, on their very existence.

Moral, Political, and Legal Human Rights

The idea of human rights, in the form we know today, emerged between the seventeenth and eighteenth centuries in the context of the American and French revolutions—1776 and 1789 respectively. They were used as political arguments against the privileges of the ancien régime, based upon the idea that all human beings, because they are human beings, have intrinsic value and hence their fundamental basic needs and interests (such as life and liberty)[6] are to be protected through fundamentally important rights. They also initiated the idea that the holders of such fundamentally important rights are themselves the reason for the existence of the state.

This emergence of human rights is what Norberto Bobbio (1988, chapter 3) refers to as a 'Copernican Revolution'—the inversion of the point of observation from the perspective of duties to the perspective of rights. He recognizes an intrinsic correlation between rights and duties, but argues that one of the two always prevails over

---

[6] On the overlap of basic interests and needs and on their relevance for the human rights discourse, see n. 91 in Pogge (1995).

or comes before the other: as a father over a son, or the head over the tail of a coin. Until the American and French revolutions, the history of human politics was characterized by the prevalence of duties over rights (Bobbio 1988). 'At the beginning ... there is always a *code of duties* (or obligations), *not of rights*' (author's translation; emphasis as per original) (Bobbio 1988: 432). Laws established what shall be done and what shall not be done for the sake of the community and, later on, the state. In this *holistic* perspective, society was the unit whose conservation and well-being came before the interest of individuals. With the Copernican Revolution, completed with the advent of constitutional democracies, this holistic perspective was replaced by an *individualistic* perception of society. The single human being assumed a value in itself, to be preserved through the respect of her rights. The state transformed from a guardian of society as a whole to a guardian of the individual and her rights.

Today, human rights are most often described as rights 'that we have simply in virtue of being human' (Griffin 2008: 2), and not because of other characteristics—race, citizenship, gender, class, and so on. All such characteristics are considered accidental and irrelevant for the recognition of human rights, which are egalitarian (the same for everyone) and universal (applicable to everyone). Human rights may come into account as moral, political, or legal concerns. Moral rights—whose existence is the object of a fierce philosophical debate—'are grounded in moral reasons [while] legal rights derive from the laws of the society' (Wenar 2011: 3). Political rights are those rights that are to be fulfilled for a political constituency to be considered as legitimate (Beitz 2003). Legal rights may or may not correspond with moral rights. The necessary correspondence between the two realms may be wished for but cannot be argued to be effective in all cases. Between legal and moral rights there is a strong, justificatory connection: moral rights provide reasons for their recognition and protection as legal rights. Such justificatory connection typically drives the historic process, leading to the genesis of new legal rights in the national and international arena.

Roughly, a moral right is used as a basis for some people to ask for the recognition of a new legal right. This aspiration could become an *opinio de iure condendo* (a proposal for the modification of existing law) of scholars, politicians, or activists, arguing that a certain moral right should be recognized in national or international law, either as the application of a new moral right or in order to give full implementation to already recognized principles or rights; the moral right may then take the form of a legal argument, which interprets certain legal texts, existing rights, court decisions, and treaties in ways consistent with the new moral right; this argumentative practice may drive the emergence of a customary norm, or eventually lead to the explicit recognition of the right in international provisions, whether non-binding, such as the UN Universal Declaration on Human Rights and the UN Declaration on the Rights of Indigenous Peoples, or binding (treaties, conventions, and covenants),[7] and in national constitutions and laws providing for its implementation and enforcement.[8] As we shall see below, by framing biocultural rights as 'emerging rights' in international law, Sanjay Bavikatte engages in the first stages of this sketched process: the creation of an opinio de iure condendo and the legal argument which frames treaties, conventions, and court cases in terms of biocultural rights.[9]

[7] A further step could be added here: the recognition of the right as *jus cogens*, a norm of international law which binds all states, regardless of whether they have explicitly agreed to it through treaty law.

[8] This description is just a rough model. It does not pretend to capture the relationships between the moral and the legal dimension of human rights in their full complexity. For example, it could also be the case that the order is reversed: the legal recognition of a human right may drive a change in common sense morality.

[9] See the subsection titled Emerging (Biocultural) Rights in Chapter 4 of this book.

Functioning and Limits of Human Rights

Trump and Balance

Human rights are commonly described as 'trumps', that is, claims used to protect individuals or groups against the excesses and degenerations of the power of the state. Human rights win over considerations of general interests because they protect human interests, which are considered fundamental to justify the change of political decisions.[10] Those individual and group interests trump the interests of the community as a whole (Dworkin 1984: 153) and lead to decisions different from those that collective goals would have led to (Waldron 1984: 17). The shift of the centre of concern from the whole to the individual or group is the core of human rights rhetoric. Their development was driven precisely by the aspiration to protect individuals and groups from limitations to their fundamental freedoms, or violations of their basic needs and interests perpetuated for the sake of the community as a whole or for the fulfilment of general values—such as the triumph of the nation, or the defence of democracy. Moreover, precisely because human rights protect very important interests, they are given special protection. They are often described as 'inalienable', that is, they cannot be waived or transferred to others, not even with the consent of their holder; 'imprescriptible', that is, they do not cease to exist, even if their holder does not exercise them or is not aware of them; and, most importantly, 'inviolable', that is, their violation is never justified.

At a first glance, it appears obvious to argue that human rights should always be treated as trumps, inviolable, imprescriptible, and inalienable vis-à-vis interests of the state, general interests of the community, or generally recognized values. Nevertheless, there might be situations of conflict between human rights and other kinds of interests, including human rights themselves, which are not obvious

---

[10] The idea of rights as trumps was developed by Dworkin (1977).

to overcome. It is possible that interests justifying two or more rights cannot be protected simultaneously or that the duties implied by two or more rights cannot be performed at the same time. In these cases, it seems inevitable to *balance* the conflicting rights (Moller 2012: 137). Balancing is the process of weighing rights against each other in order to decide which one should prevail over the other and to what extent each shall be restricted. Surely, it could be objected that balancing is just a rhetorical technique, which could hide value decisions under the cloak of correctness—'it is nothing more than an arbitrary and rash Solomonic settlement,' some may say (Pulido 2006: 195). But human rights are the results of complex historical and cultural processes that reflect heterogeneous values, ideals, and interests in a context in which resources are limited. They are not the product of a rational system created to be comprehensive and coherent, and even if they are conceived as a self-standing whole, as in the case of biocultural rights, balance may need to be sought between their very foundations. Hence, the balancing of rights is, though some kind of a defeat, a strict necessity.

Conflicts may also arise between human rights and the general interest of the state, the community, or a generally recognized value. One might say that of course human rights trump such interests, otherwise they would not be human rights. But if this were the case we would have to admit that most constitutions and international treaties do not, in fact, contain real human rights. Article 29 of the Universal Declaration on Human Rights, for example, conditions, in exceptional circumstances, the exercise of rights and freedoms to limitations aimed at securing the rights and freedoms of others and meeting the requirements of morality, public order, and general welfare in a democratic society.

Does this mean that human rights are not real trumps? Not necessarily. It means that they are very important moral and legal concerns, so important that they *usually* trump general interests or values. They might need to be limited, however, when extremely serious, important and exceptional considerations arise.

Vis-à-vis General Interest

As explained above, the human rights discourse usually builds on the idea that human rights foundations, the reasons which justify their ascription, lie in the intrinsic value of the right holder (may it be a person or group of people). This value is conceived as irreducible to, and diverging from, general interests of the community as a whole. General interests may, in fact, provide reasons both in favour of, and in conflict with, the protection and promotion of such intrinsic value, but they are always *extrinsic* to the right, not part of its structure.[11]

An example might clarify this crucial point. Freedom of expression is commonly understood to be a human right. It safeguards the intrinsic value of every person by protecting his or her fundamental interest in expressing ideas and communicating with other people. Importantly, we also know that if applied well, freedom of expression can *also* promote the general interest of the growth of knowledge and culture. However, such general interest appears to be extrinsic to the right: it does not provide one of its foundations. It simply is a further

[11] The idea that human rights are grounded in the intrinsic value of human persons and groups is deeply embedded in the human rights discourse. It is not, however, unanimously accepted by scholars. According to the *instrumental* conception, the ascription of rights—even particularly 'protected rights such as those usually labelled 'human rights'—can only be justified as a way of maximizing general utility; for a brief introduction see Wenar (2011). According to the *political* conception, human rights are not moral entities, but political ones. They are rights that 'set the limits to the sovereignty of states', and are a sufficient reason to act against violations in the international arena, even at the cost of the sovereignty of a state; see Raz (2010: 328). This conception rests on the assumption that human rights do not belong to people solely by virtue of their being human and are dependent on national and international law; see Beitz (2003: 43) and Raz (2010: 336).

benefit society may obtain from the realization of the right. In fact, we do not think that only those people who are likely to exercise the right in ways that contribute to the growth of knowledge are entitled to it. Neither do we think that the recognition of the right should be submitted to empirical tests controlling whether it actually leads to a general increase of knowledge and culture. If someone was entitled to decide which books, speeches, videos, and the like, provide a growth of knowledge and may hence be made public, or if someone was to decide whether freedom of expression should be generally restricted in order to pursue the growth of knowledge, we would not welcome this practice as being in line with the very logic of the freedom of expression. Rather, we would consider it a serious violation of that same right to freedom of expression.

If conditioning the freedom of expression in this way seems unacceptable, it is because we regard the interest of every person to be free to communicate as the proper foundation of this right, its raison d'être, and not the general interest in the growth of knowledge. It is important to note that such considerations also concern the limits that the general interest might constitute to a right. For example, we accept that freedom of movement may be limited in exceptional circumstances for the sake of the general interest. If an epidemic of an infectious disease occurs, freedom of movement could endanger greater and greater parts of the population and could, for this reason, be restricted. However, we would not regard this restriction as stemming from the very logic of freedom of movement. The maintenance of public safety and health do not appear to be a conceptual limit intrinsic to freedom of movement, as if they were part of the reasons why the latter is recognized as a human right. On the contrary, they appear to be an external consideration of general interests that, when certain extreme circumstances materialize, may restrict the realization of the right.

Let us briefly sum up the main points emerging from this (rough) reconstruction of the notion of human rights embedded in moral, political, and legal discourse. According to this notion, a human right is grounded in the protection of very important interests of a person (or group of people), which is considered to have intrinsic value. These interests are the foundations of the right and provide it with a special normative force: it defeats general interests—apart from exceptional circumstances—and it imposes upon states and the international community the duty to provide it with a legal acknowledgement and to assure it a certain degree of protection.

In Bavikatte's work, biocultural rights are considered as human rights: grounded in very important interests of indigenous peoples and local communities and having a special normative force. They are not already existing human rights, but potentially emerging ones in international law. As we shall see, however, they are sui generis human rights because they host a general interest, conservation of the environment, as one of their foundations, with very challenging implications.

Beyond the Individual

Universality and Specialization

The practice and rhetoric of human rights has evolved in ways that have partially overcome their above-mentioned egalitarian façade and universality. This evolution can be described as zigzagging steps that begin with claims for universality and end with the current specialization (Bobbio 1988). Initially, in seventeenth-century Europe, the human rights theory aimed at abolishing differences between citizens and non-citizens, and between people belonging to different social classes, declaring all human beings (or at least all those at that time perceived as such) holders of the same *universal* human rights. Then, at the end of the eighteenth century, during the American and French revolutions, human rights became legal rights, embedded in constitutions, and therefore somehow lost their universality to be restricted to citizens only. After World War II, and in particular, since the adoption of the Universal Declaration of Human Rights (1948) and the UN International Covenant on Civil and Political Rights (1966), and International Covenant on Economic, Social and Cultural Rights (1966)—which recognize rights to 'all members of the human family' as inherently holders of dignity—human rights encountered a new wave of universalization. A wide set of rights entered the international debate as, at least in theory, universally applicable to all human beings. It became part of the global political agenda and turned into standards for assessments, criticism, aspiration, and evaluation of political and economic organizations to the point of becoming a *global* concern (Beitz 2003: 44).[12] The last of these steps consists in the important re-emergence of *differences* in the human rights rhetoric. At the international as well as national level differences became the justification for the recognition of *special* rights to certain categories of holders of specific needs which protect very important interests essential for their dignity and personhood—the most important being UN Conventions Relating to the Status of Refugees (1951), on the Elimination of all Forms of Discrimination against Women (1979), on the Rights of the Child (1989), and on the Rights of Persons with Disabilities (2007). This progressive recognition of special human rights to specific categories of people builds on the understanding that equal consideration for all cannot be reached by according the same rights to everyone, because certain people have, or find themselves in, conditions which do not allow them to fully enjoy basic and universal human rights like other people unless specific support is provided.

Introducing Group Rights

The *universality* of human rights is an object of a wide debate, since many people challenge the idea that human rights are independent

---

[12] See also Beitz (2001: 269).

from epoch, culture, and place, and that they are only and always individual-centred. Hence, the critiques to the universalism of human rights do not end with the recognition of differentiated rights for specific categories of human beings. One important issue of human rights concerns the question of whether it is appropriate to talk about human rights in the global arena, where cultures[13] are very heterogeneous and necessarily differ from Western culture, where the concept of human rights is said to have evolved.[14] The debate between *universalists* and *relativists*, between those that believe in the existence of a universal moral code common to all humanity, and those who find different rightful moral codes in different communities, times, and places, is highly controversial. While the first advocate for the recognition and application of human rights to all human beings regardless of their community of origin, religion, ethnicity, and culture, the second question this attitude as yet another pattern of cultural imperialism and forced assimilation.

The debate of the two sides is particularly relevant for indigenous peoples and local communities, as they have often found themselves at the border between the two positions. While human rights rhetoric is widely practised by their representatives, claims against cultural imperialism and forced assimilation are essential in their struggles. Ronald Niezen (2003) suggests that the engagement of indigenous peoples in a global movement for the recognition of rights may be regarded as a political strategy to fight the political, economic, and cultural dominance of states. According to him, indigenous peoples

---

[13] 'Culture' is a term that has been defined in many different ways, often depending on the scientific context. In this book, it is used to describe the heritage of knowledge, values, customs, beliefs, world views, and legal systems of a community.

[14] There is wide existing literature on this important point by postcolonial scholars, such as Baxi (2002: 33), who challenges the idea that human rights are 'a gift of the West to the rest'.

have learnt to use Western instruments and speak in their language, that is, the language of written law and human rights, to support their claims. This strategy, which 'entails almost as much cultural transition as cultural preservation' (Niezen 2003: 118), has also contributed to the evolution of the human rights rhetoric and structure in ways that are more appropriate to answer to the needs of indigenous peoples.

As we saw above, human rights were born as individual rights accorded to *all* individuals, regardless of their characteristics, and as single, self-standing, entities. Indigenous peoples have 'challenge[d] the exclusively individualistic approach to human rights and stand apart from the usual prescription of human rights on the basis of individual protection' (Niezen 2003: 118). Their claims have focused predominantly on group rights, as an instrument for the protection of certain interests that are specific and necessary for their survival, identity, and flourishing. Group rights are 'rights held by a group as a group rather than by its members severally' (Jones 2014: 1), and they must not be confused with the rights held only by the members of a certain category of individuals and not by the rest of humankind. Hence, for example, most women's rights (such as the right to maternity leave) are not rights of women as a group but rather are individual rights ascribed to a category of people who share certain characteristics considered relevant for the entitlement of certain rights. The relevance of their special rights does not stem from them being a group, but rather from them being individuals with particular characteristics.

Group rights instead are justified as necessary for the protection of the group per se, because it is perceived to have intrinsic value.[15] Certain group rights might be reducible to the interests of their individual members—and are hence justified also on the basis of protection of their individual intrinsic value—while others, such as the

---

[15] See the subsection titled, 'A Matter of Value' in Chapter 1 of this book.

right to self-determination, belong to the group because it has interests that are not the mere aggregation of the interests of its members.[16] The right to self-determination, for instance, has a different meaning depending on whether it is attributed to a community or to a person. An individual right to self-determination concerns the right to determine the path of one's life. The right to self-determination of a group, instead, concerns the control over the destiny of the collective life of the group, not the mere sum of the lives of its members (Jones 2014: 2). If a member of the group (self-)determines to leave the group, she is not exercising the right to self-determination of the group, but her own right. If the assembly or the legitimate leader of the group (self-) determines to dismiss the group, or to change its name or location, or to adopt new rules, they are exercising the right to self-determination of the group and are doing things that no single member has the right to do.

It should be noted that if groups have rights not reducible to the rights of their members, then these two sets of rights may be in conflict and the rights of the individuals within the group may, in certain instances, be threatened (Hartney 1995: 209). One of the first instances that come to mind is the potential violation of the individual rights of women by the group.[17] This issue has been discussed extensively for what concerns indigenous peoples (Nagengast 1997), as, in some cases, indigenous women have themselves raised the fear that

----

[16] Michael Hartney argues the opposite. For him, all group rights are reducible to individual rights. The right to self-determination is a good to be preserved because it benefits the members of the group whose self-determination is recognized. Hartney (1995: 206–8) argues that 'only the lives of individual human beings have ultimate value, and [therefore] collective entities derive their value from their contribution to the lives of individual human beings'.

[17] See Deveaux (2000); Okin (1999).

an increased self-determination of the group might endanger their individual rights.[18]

One way to overcome these potential conflicts and protect the centrality of individual rights is to view group rights (especially when dealing with non-voluntary groups whose membership is not chosen, such as ethnic and linguistic groups) predominantly as rights directed outward (as protection from other groups, and the state), rather than inward (towards the members of the groups).[19] Accordingly, group rights should remain subject to the individual rights of their

[18] See, amongst others, Kuokkanen (2012: 238), who suggests that, in certain cases, 'it appears that for the indigenous self-determination movement, violence against women is considered neither an indigenous rights issue nor a human rights issue'. Among the many controversies, see, for example, Deveaux (2000: 527) on the fear of many Canadian native and first nations women that they would lose the 'existing protections of sex equality rights as guaranteed by federal Canadian law' if indigenous governments were recognized independent of an overarching Canadian law, including the Canadian Charter of Rights and Freedoms, and Sylvain (2011: 101), who describes the struggles of San women in the Omaheke Region in central-east Namibia and argues that there is a 'possibility that collective rights to political representation under the Traditional Authorities Act may serve to reinforce gender inequalities within communities'.

[19] Kymlicka (1994) distinguishes between two categories of rights aiming at protecting the stability and self-preservation of a cultural or ethnic community: group rights and special rights. The first category protects communities from internal dissent and the second from external dissent. Group rights are rights that communities have as community, independently from the interests of the members of the community. The community is described as a self-standing entity, whose existence and flourishing has a value per se and, therefore, deserves protection. Special rights instead, Kymlicka argues, are rights of certain people as members of a certain group. They can also have the form of individual rights and regulate inter-group relations: special

members: first, the right to exit, to leave the group;[20] second, all other individual rights necessary to protect individuals against the domination and discrimination of group's authority, as stated in international human rights law or national bills of rights and constitutions.[21]

Overall, and in many circumstances, group rights are an instrument that can protect and uphold particularly important group interests more adequately than individual rights. Some confusion has arisen over which groups are entitled to become rights holders, as not all gatherings of people (such as those queuing at a post office) can be considered to have a value worthy of legal protection through the instrument of human rights. The type of group that is most commonly argued to have value is an ethnic minority, because ethnic minorities endorse the flourishing of cultural diversity, which is considered to be highly valuable (Anaya 1997). Additionally, ethnic minorities often find themselves in particularly vulnerable positions, hence, the 'effective realization of equality requires in many instances differential treatment of ethnic groups in ways not necessary for, or even relevant to, other types of groups' (Anaya 1997: 223).

Indigenous peoples and certain local communities are a particular type of ethnic group and are hence entitled to become holders of group rights. As the reader will have noted, the concept of biocultural rights refers to both indigenous peoples and local communities. Bavikatte

---

rights 'compensate for unequal circumstances which put the members of minority cultures at a systemic disadvantage in the whole marketplace, regardless of their personal choices in life' (Kymlicka 1994: 25).

[20] According to Susan Okin (2002: 206), the right to exit cannot be considered sufficient to protect women's rights within groups because they 'are far less than men to be able to exercise the right of exit'.

[21] For an extensive treatment of the possible ways to overcome—or dismiss—the clash between group rights and women rights, see the responses to Okin's essay, 'Is Multiculturalism Bad for Women?' in Okin (1999).

(2014: 1, n. 1) gathers the two groups under the same umbrella of rights, making no specific distinction between them.[22] However, the border between the two terms is very important. They are different subjects in international and national law, on whom different rights have been bestowed so far. The following sections in this chapter will draw a sketch of the two subjects—indigenous peoples and local communities—in order to prepare the stage for discussing the complications linked with the rhetoric of biocultural rights and the rights of indigenous peoples.

Two Special Types of Group Rights

Rights of Indigenous Peoples

Most papers, books, and reports regarding indigenous peoples affirm that there are more than 370 million people living in 90 different countries that may be called indigenous (UN 2009). This estimate is problematic not only because of the lack of a regular and systematic national census of indigenous peoples but also because of the yet unresolved difficulties concerning the definition of the term itself (Niezen 2003: 224). Currently, there is no universally recognized definition, but several different ones, which are only partly overlapping. The most widely known is the one proposed by Martínez Cobo in the *Study of the Problem of Discrimination Against Indigenous Populations*,[23]

---

[22] The relevance of the difference between indigenous peoples and local communities *vis-à-vis* the idea of biocultural rights is elaborated in the subsection titled, 'Indigenous Peoples or Local Communities—A Necessary Distinction' in Chapter 5 of this book.

[23] Martínez Cobo was the Special Rapporteur of the Sub-Commission on Prevention of Discrimination and Protection of Minorities. The study was the first extensive research commissioned by the UN on the indigenous issue and was adopted at the 52nd meeting of the UN Economic and Social Council, on 11 March 1986.

commissioned by the UN in 1986. According to UN Commission on Human Rights (1986: para 379),

> Indigenous communities, peoples and nations are those which, having a historical continuity with pre-invasion and pre-colonial societies that developed on their territories, consider themselves distinct from other sectors of the societies now prevailing in those territories, or parts of them. They form at present non-dominant sectors of society and are determined to preserve, develop and transmit to future generations their ancestral territories, and their ethnic identity, as the basis of their continued existence as peoples, in accordance with their own cultural patterns, social institutions and legal systems.

In 2007, the UN General Assembly (UNGA) adopted the Declaration on the Rights of Indigenous Peoples (UNDRIP). Rather than providing a strict definition, which may be in danger of excluding certain peoples who deserve to be considered indigenous, the UNDRIP suggests, in different articles, some key characteristics of indigenous peoples which should guide their identification with some flexibility:[24] self-identification as indigenous peoples;[25]

---

[24] The peculiar features of indigenous cultures, institutions, and traditions have also been central in the description of indigenous peoples in the 1989 International Labour Organization (ILO) Convention Number 169 on Indigenous and Tribal Peoples' Rights: Article 1 says, 'Tribal peoples in independent countries whose social, cultural and economic conditions distinguish them from other sections of the national community, and whose status is regulated wholly or partially by their own customs or traditions or by special laws or regulations.' ILO Convention 169 is a treaty which has so far been signed by 22 states: Argentina, Bolivia, Brazil, Central African Republic, Chile, Colombia, Costa Rica, Denmark, Dominica, Ecuador, Fiji, Guatemala, Honduras, Mexico, Nepal, Netherlands, Nicaragua, Norway, Paraguay, Peru, Spain, and the Bolivarian Republic of Venezuela.

[25] UNDRIP, Article 33.

a history of common injustices as a result of colonization and land dispossession;[26] language, traditional practices, knowledge, and legal and cultural institutions distinct from those dominant in the national state where they reside;[27] and knowledge, culture, and practices that contribute to the sustainable use and management of the environment.[28] Drawing on the characteristic features used in the different definitions, the term 'indigenous peoples' refers to those peoples that self-identify as indigenous, that are linked to precolonial societies and that present a combination of the following characteristics: strong link to a certain land and its natural resources; cultural, legal, spiritual, and economic traditions different from mainstream society; determination to preserve, develop, and transmit distinct traditions and lands; past, and often present, marginalization and oppression.

Importantly, the UNDRIP refers to indigenous *peoples*, in plural, because *peoples* are recognized as subjects of international law, and in particular as subjects whose right to self-determination is recognized by the two 1966 international covenants on civil and political rights, and economic, social, and cultural rights.[29] The right to self-determination 'symbolizes not just the basic human rights to which all individuals are entitled, but also land, territorial and collective rights, subsumed

[26]   UNDRIP, Preamble.

[27]   UNDRIP, Articles 5, 11, 12, 13, 20, 27, 31, and 34.

[28]   UNDRIP, Preamble.

[29]   Article 1 in both the covenants states:

1. All peoples have the right of self-determination. By virtue of that right they freely determine their political status and freely pursue their economic, social and cultural development. 2. All peoples may, for their own ends, freely dispose of their natural wealth and resources without prejudice to any obligations arising out of international economic co-operation, based upon the principle of mutual benefit, and international law. In no case may a people be deprived of its own means of subsistence.

under the right to self-determination' (Posey 1999a: 4). Unfortunately historically, self-determination has been associated with secessionism, militaristic and peace-threatening ethno-nationalism, and conflicts between minorities (Anaya 1996: 98, n. 4). Many states have expressed the fear that recognition of the right to self-determination to indigenous peoples may pose a threat to their territorial integrity (Xanthaki 2007: 140). For this reason, advocates of indigenous rights have underlined that indigenous peoples have been asking for a different type of self-determination, one which does not entail secession and independence (Xanthaki 2007: 146). Indigenous peoples have been claiming *internal* self-determination, which is aimed at asserting identities, preserving languages, cultures, and practices, and at maintaining traditional governance structures (Anaya 1996: 111).

Accordingly, the UNDRIP, as well as Convention 169 on Indigenous and Tribal Peoples of the International Labour Organization (ILO 169), describe the right to self-determination of indigenous peoples as the right to determine their political status and pursue their economic, social, and cultural development goals without the need to create independent states,[30] and as the prerequisite for the realization of the indigenous 'right to be equal but different':[31] that is, the right to maintain cultural, religious, and economic traditions and social institutions separate from those of the dominant part of the society. For the realization of the right to self-determination of indigenous peoples, the recognition of rights to their lands, territories, and natural resources is paramount (Anaya 1996: 104). The UNDRIP and ILO 169 recognize

---

[30] Article 3 of the UNDRIP suggests ways of understanding self-determination, in line with the ILO Convention 169, whose Preamble recognizes indigenous aspirations 'to exercise control over their own institutions, ways of life and economic development and to maintain and develop their identities, languages and religions, within the framework of the States in which they live'.

[31] UNDRIP, Article 2.

the right of indigenous peoples to the lands, territories, and natural resources they have traditionally owned, occupied or used, specifically acknowledging traditional occupation or use as title.[32] Rights to lands, territories, and resources also include the right to maintain distinctive spiritual traditions, customs, and land tenure systems,[33] and the right to conservation and protection of the environment of their lands and territories.[34]

The UNDRIP, underlining that indigenous peoples have been, and still are, extensively dispossessed of their lands, territories, and resources, calls states to provide effective mechanisms for prevention of forced removals and relocations, and, when this is not possible, to provide redress or compensation.[35] Furthermore, they are accorded the right to free prior informed consent in all cases when their lands and natural resources might be affected by state's adoption or implementation of legislative and administrative measures and projects.[36] Free prior informed consent entails the right of the people affected by an activity to be fully informed, before commencement, about the aims of the action, its procedure, timings, and potential costs and benefits. Indigenous peoples have also stressed the importance of recognizing not only their right to be fully informed but also their right to freely refuse to provide consent.

[32] UNDRIP, Article 26 and, accordingly, ILO Convention 169, Articles 14–17.

[33] UNDRIP, Articles 25 and 27, and of ILO Convention 169, Articles 2b and 7.

[34] UNDRIP, Article 29.

[35] UNDRIP, Article 28.

[36] UNDRIP, Article 19: 'States shall consult and cooperate in good faith with the indigenous peoples concerned through their own representative institutions in order to obtain their free, prior and informed consent before adopting and implementing legislative or administrative measures that may affect them.' See also, UNDRIP, Article 32.2 and ILO Convention 196, Article 6.

The right to self-determination, so heterogeneously composed, is the foundation upon which the realization of all other indigenous rights is based. It can be said to encompass—and be the prerequisite for the fulfilment of—indigenous peoples' rights to non-discrimination, cultural integrity, and social welfare and development (Anaya 1996: 97). Non-discrimination is the foundation of the protection of the rights of all minority groups (Bloch 2001: 376) because it builds on the assumption that only through the recognition of such rights can minorities be assured to have de facto equal protection of their interests, needs, and identity and 'for the preservation of those characteristics and traditions which distinguish them from the majority of the population' (Bloch 2011: 377).

The right to non-discrimination is recognized in most international declarations and conventions on human rights: the Universal Declaration on Human Rights, two international covenants of 1966, International Convention on the Elimination of All Forms of Racial Discrimination, UN Declaration on the Rights of Minorities, and UNDRIP. The last convention recognizes the right of indigenous peoples to be free from discrimination of any kind,[37] with particular reference to exercise—without discrimination—their rights to education, access to media, fair and just labour conditions, health, conservation and protection of the environment, and development and use of their lands and territories.[38] The right to non-discrimination is strongly linked to the right to cultural integrity, which addresses the need of every person to take part in the cultural life of her own community, to participate in its development, to use and practise its language, religion, art, customs, and scientific and literary production.[39]

---

[37] UNDRIP, Preamble and Articles 2 and 15.

[38] UNDRIP, Articles 14, 16, 17, 24, 29, and 32.

[39] These rights are listed in Article 27 of the Universal Declaration of Human Rights; Article 15 of the International Covenant on Economic,

In particular, the UNDRIP calls for the respect of indigenous cultural heritage, which includes knowledge of lands and their natural components, practices, arts, literature, religion, rites, philosophy, and demands that states respect and protect heritage from forced assimilation.[40]

Indigenous peoples have also been granted the rights to welfare and development. Welfare entails those economic and social rights—such as the rights to health, to an adequate standard of living, to education, to live in a healthy environment—needed to survive, flourish, and maintain and develop traditional practices essential to the culture of any ethnic community (Bloch 2001: 379). The UNDRIP specifies the right to use traditional medicines and health practices, which includes the right to the conservation of medicinal plants, animals, and minerals.[41] These rights are the basis for the realization of the right to development defined by the UN Declaration on the Right to Development as the right to 'participate in, contribute to, and enjoy

Social and Cultural Rights; Article 13c of the Convention on the Elimination of All Forms of Discrimination against Women; Article 31 of the Convention on the Rights of the Child; and Article 4 of the UN Declaration on the Rights of Persons Belonging to National or Ethnic, Religious and Linguistic Minorities.

[40] Articles 8, 11, 12, 13, and 14. Article 31 of the UNDRIP states:

   1. Indigenous peoples have the right to maintain, control, protect and develop their cultural heritage, traditional knowledge and traditional cultural expressions, as well as the manifestations of their sciences, technologies and cultures, including human and genetic resources, seeds, medicines, knowledge of the properties of fauna and flora, oral traditions, literatures, designs, sports and traditional games and visual and performing arts. They also have the right to maintain, control, protect and develop their intellectual property over such cultural heritage, traditional knowledge, and traditional cultural expressions.

[41] UNDRIP, Article 24.

economic, social, cultural and political development, in which all human rights and fundamental freedoms can be fully realized'.[42] The UNDRIP interprets the right to development as particularly centred on the right for indigenous peoples to determine and freely and autonomously develop their priorities and strategies for the development of their lands, territories, and resources,[43] as well as the right to be included in state-led development projects without discrimination.[44]

Besides the UNDRIP, which remains a non-binding declaration, indigenous peoples have been granted rights by other conventions and declarations, such as the CBD and the Nagoya Protocol on Access to Genetic Resources and the Fair and Equitable Sharing of the Benefits Arising from their Utilization, which is explored further in Chapter 4.

Rights of Local Communities

The definition of 'local communities' has not undergone as extensive an analysis as the term 'indigenous peoples'. Their first acknowledgement in international law is found in Article 8j of the CBD (Jonas, Makagon, and Shrumm 2013: 24). The CBD, echoing principle 22 of the Rio Declaration,[45] addresses 'indigenous and local communities

---

[42] UN Declaration on the Right to Development, Article 1.

[43] UNDRIP, Articles 23 and 32.

[44] UNDRIP, Articles 21 and 24.

[45] The Rio Declaration was adopted at the UN Conference on Environment and Development, also known as the Earth Summit, in Rio de Janeiro in 1992. Principle 22 of the Rio Declaration states: 'Indigenous people and their communities and other local communities have a vital role in environmental management and development because of their knowledge and traditional practices. States should recognize and duly support their identity, culture and interests and enable their effective participation in the achievement of sustainable development.'

embodying traditional lifestyles relevant for the conservation of the environment'[46] as holders of rights over their traditional knowledge associated with genetic resources. The term local community has since appeared in many other international documents issued by UN bodies, UN treaties, and other international organizations, for example, in the 2010 Nagoya Protocol to the CBD, the 2006 International Tropical Timber Agreement, the 2001 Food and Agriculture Organization International Treaty on Plant Genetic Resources for Food and Agriculture, the 1995 Agreement for the Implementation of the UN Convention on the Law of the Sea, the 1994 Convention to Combat Desertification, resolutions of the Conference of the Parties and Guidelines of the 1971 Ramsar Convention on Wetlands (Bessa 2015: 332–4), resolutions, policy documents, and guidelines of the International Union for the Conservation of Nature (IUCN) and the World Wide Fund for Nature (WWF) (Borrini-Feyerabend, Kothari, and Oviedo 2004: 12).

In all these documents, local communities are taken into account because of their relationship with the environment, whether this means lands, seeds, trees, animals, plants, rivers, deserts, or wet and dry lands. They do not come into play in the rights discourse simply because of their existence as communities, but precisely because of their role in the conservation of important natural resources (Jonas, Makagon, and Shrumm 2013: 26). In 2011, the CBD Conference of the Parties convened an ad hoc expert meeting to shed some light on the use of the term, determining the core characteristics of local communities (UNEP 2011). The list that was agreed upon is 'broad and inclusive, and allow[s] for a clustering of unique cultural, ecological and social circumstances to each community' (Jonas, Makagon, and Shrumm 2013: 25). Many of the listed characteristics are very similar to those used to identify indigenous peoples: self-identification; strong

----

[46] CBD, Article 8j.

link to traditional lands; set of cultural (including linguistic), legal, spiritual, and economic traditions different from mainstream society; dynamic and evolving traditional practices and knowledge passed from generation to generation; past, and often present, marginalization and oppression (UNEP 2011: 12–13).

Besides these common characteristics, the CBD expert meeting kept the focus on the importance of environmental sustainability. The working group suggested that in order to be classified as a 'local community', a community needs to have 'lifestyles linked to traditions associated with natural cycles', to be involved in 'sustainable use of nature and biodiversity', and to hold 'technology/knowledge/innovations/practices associated with the sustainable use and conservation of biological diversity', 'spiritual and cultural values of biodiversity and territories', and 'foods and food preparation systems and traditional medicines ... closely connected to biodiversity/environment' (UNEP 2011: 12–13). As a result, the CBD expert meeting might have somehow blurred the distinction between the definition of 'local communities' and the requirements they need to fulfil to be *holders of certain rights*. For the purposes of this book, it is more appropriate to dissociate the two concepts: that is, the definition of local communities, and the characteristics they need to have in order to qualify as holders of certain rights granted only to those local communities that have environmentally sound practices and lifestyles. The definition of local communities used here, hence, does not include environmental sustainability as a prerequisite, and only focuses on sociocultural characteristics: rural groups of people that 'do not fit the strict test of indigeneity but nevertheless' (Bessa 2015: 332) identify themselves as a community, who live with low population densities and regulate themselves by their own norms and traditions, who have a long-standing social and cultural organization that binds them together to a defined land and its natural resources, which distinguishes them from other, more affirmed and less marginalized, sectors of society.

Notwithstanding the CBD's attempt to identify local communities, the question of what local communities and their differentiated rights are remains a complex and nuanced one. The Inter-American Court of Human Rights[47] has recently issued two widely discussed judgments concerning the rights of local communities. In the two cases, the Court treated local communities as holders of the same rights as indigenous peoples (Antkowiak 2007). Specifically, in the 2005 case of *Moiwana Village v. Suriname*,[48] the Court recognized the Moiwana local community, composed of descendants of African slaves who escaped and settled in the late nineteenth century, as the legitimate owner of its ancestral territory, regardless of the lack of legal title.[49] The Court followed the same rationale used in the case of *Mayagna (Sumo) Awas Tingni Community v. Nicaragua*,[50] which instead dealt with indigenous peoples, arguing that 'in the case of indigenous communities who have occupied their ancestral lands in accordance with customary practices—yet who lack real title to the property—mere possession of the land should suffice to obtain official recognition of their communal ownership.'[51] Equally, in the 2007 case of *Saramaka People v. Suriname*,[52] the Inter-American Court recognized to the Saramaka people, also descendants of African slaves, the collective ownership of

---

[47] The Inter-American Court of Human Rights, together with the Inter-American Commission on Human Rights, safeguards the American Convention on Human Rights. The Convention was adopted by the Organization of American States and entered into force in 1978.

[48] Inter-Am. C.H.R., No. 124, Ser. C (2005) (hereinafter referred to as *Moiwana Village*).

[49] *Moiwana Village*, paras 128, 132.

[50] Inter-Am. C.H.R., No. 79, Ser. C (2001) (hereinafter referred to as *Mayagna (Sumo) Awas Tingni Community*).

[51] *Moiwana Village*, para 131.

[52] Inter-Am. C.H.R., No. 172, Ser. C (2007) (hereinafter referred to as *Saramaka People*).

their ancestral land, by applying its precedents regarding indigenous peoples 'because both share distinct social, cultural, and economic characteristics, including a special relationship with their ancestral territories, that require special measures under international human rights law in order to guarantee their physical and cultural survival'.[53]

Notwithstanding these decisions and the many common characteristics of local communities and indigenous peoples, they remain two distinct subjects under international law, whose legal rights are profoundly different. This caveat is important in the discussion about biocultural rights, as will be further clarified in Chapter 5.

[53] *Saramaka People*, para 86.

3 Friends and Foes

Rights, the Environment, and People

Human Rights and the Environment

The Environment for Rights

Protection of the environment is essential for the fulfilment of human rights (Bosselmann 2015: 531)—and in particular for the rights of indigenous peoples and local communities.[1] In 1968, the UNGA for the first time formally recognized the interdependence of environmental protection and basic human rights,[2]

---

[1] Francesco Francioni, for example, underlines the relevance given to the environment in the UNDRIP and in the African Charter on Human and Peoples' Rights; see Francioni (2010: 43).

[2] Resolution 2398 (XXII), cited in Sands et al. (2012: 777).

and four years later, in the Stockholm Declaration adopted at the UN Conference on Human Environment, conservation of the environment was presented as essential to human well-being and 'to the enjoyment of basic human rights—even the right to life itself' (UN 1972: Preamble). For the last 30 years, human rights and environmental protection have been understood as 'interrelated fundamental goals of the global community' (Greiber 2009: 5). In 2009, the UN High Commissioner for Human Rights (UNHCHR) pointed out that 'while the universal human rights treaties do not refer to a specific right to a safe and healthy environment, the United Nations human rights treaty bodies all recognize the intrinsic link between the environment and the realization of a range of human rights'.[3] And in 2012, the UN appointed the independent expert on human rights obligations relating to the enjoyment of a safe, clean, healthy, and sustainable environment—then reassigned in 2015 as Special Rapporteur on Human Rights and the Environment—endorsing the relevance of the issue for the international community at large. Accordingly, the new 2016 development goals incorporate the idea that economic and social growth need to go hand in hand with protection of the environment, thus moving from the previous (Millennium) Development Goals to Sustainable Development Goals.

To picture how environmental harm can damage the fulfilment of fundamental rights of individuals and groups and limit the exercise of their fundamental freedoms (Lewis 2012a: 38) even looking at only a few human rights is sufficient, as they can clearly have no fulfilment without a certain quality of the environment. Overexploitation and land degradation increase environmental hazards, threatening the

---

[3] See the report of the Office of the High Commissioner for Human Rights (OHCHR) on the relationship between climate change and human rights, UN Doc. A/HRC/10/61, 15 January 2009, para 18, cited in Boyle (2012: 617).

right to life and security of the person,[4] and, consequently, the right to family life.[5] If air, soil, and water are polluted there can be no respect towards the right to a standard of living adequate for health, to the healthy development of the child,[6] to hygiene,[7] to well-being,[8] and to a healthy work environment,[9] nor can there be respect towards the right to food.[10] To fulfil the latter it is also necessary to conserve a certain level of biodiversity as it is key for food security (World Resources Institute 2005). Therefore, 'soil depletion, deforestation, overexploitation, and pollution represent a direct threat to' (World Resources Institute 2005: 13) human rights and contribute to the maintenance and exacerbation of poverty. There can neither be a realization of the right to participate in social and cultural activities,[11] nor to profess religion,[12] if pollution, wastes, and ecosystem degradation make access to natural sites impossible or dangerous. Environmental degradation appears to be particularly harmful for indigenous peoples and local communities, for whom lands and natural resources play a fundamental role in the economic, social, cultural, and spirituals aspects of their lives and livelihoods (Lewis 2012b: 67–8). Among the fundamental rights potentially violated by environmental degradation their rights to self-determination and development stand out clearly, as they are depend on lands and natural resources that

---

[4] Recognized in the UDHR, Article 3, and ICCPR, Articles 6(1) and 9(1).

[5] UDHR, Article 16(3); ICCPR, Article 23; 1966 ICESCR, Article 10(1).

[6] ICESCR, Article 12(2)(a).

[7] ICESCR, Article 12(2)(b).

[8] UDHR, Article 25(1); ICESCR, Article 12(1).

[9] UDHR, Article 23; ICESCR Article 7b.

[10] ICESCR, Article 11.

[11] UDHR, Article 27(1); ICESCR, Article 15(1).

[12] ICCPR, Article 18(1).

are not polluted, exhausted, or extinct.[13] Equally, the right to enjoy culture, religion, and language[14] are intrinsically linked to environmental assets, as well as the most basic rights to well-being, an adequate standard of living, and physical and mental health (Lewis 2012b: 68).

Rights for the Environment

That said, vis-à-vis the current environmental crisis[15] the discourse on human rights needs to incorporate the recognition of the scarcity of the earth's resources and of the vulnerability of its ecosystems. The crisis requires us to reshape the 'traditional thinking on human rights' (Bosselmann 2015: 531) and proposals such as the introduction of the right to a clean and healthy environment are examples of efforts to integrate conservation of the environment with human rights rhetoric. Literature and courts have been quite active in addressing this need for change. When trying to classify the different responses that have been proposed, it is possible to distinguish three modes of incorporation of the environment in human rights theory and law: the greening of human rights, the development of procedural environmental rights, and the creation of specific environmental human rights (Taylor 2008: 94–8).

The 'greening' of human rights reflects the increasing understanding that the fulfilment of many human rights requires a healthy environment, as described above. In cases where human rights—such as the right to health, to life, to development, and to family life—are violated by environmental degradation, courts ruling in favour of human rights protection have started to halt

[13] ICCPR, Article 1; ICESCR, Article 1.

[14] ICCPR, Article 27.

[15] See the section titled 'Facing Responsibilities' in Chapter 1 of this book.

environmentally harming activity, such as the pollution of a river with toxic chemicals (Taylor 1998: 338–43).

Procedural environmental rights, instead, reflect the fact that not only human rights realization benefits from a well-preserved and healthy environment, but also that the conservation of environment can be better supported when human rights are realized. Procedural environmental rights are counted among civil and political rights, such as the right to information, participation, protest, and free prior informed consent. Those rights have been interpreted as providing rights relevant for the environment, such as the right to information regarding environmental impact assessments of new private and state projects and actions.[16] A well-functioning democratic state where fundamental civil and political rights are recognized and upheld is more likely to listen and respond to environment-related demands of its citizens (Lewis 2012a: 39).[17] Environmental activism does, for example, benefit from civil and political rights (Gearty 2010: 15–17), as the killing of increasing number of activists in countries where these rights have little protection demonstrates (Global Witness 2015).

[16] In other cases, specific environmental procedural rights have been recognized, for example, through the European Union Aarhus Convention on Access to Information, Public Participation in Decision-Making and Access to Justice in Environmental Matters. The Aarhus Convention came into force in 2001 and adopts a rights-based approach to environmental issues. It recognizes the right to access to environmental information, the right to public participation in environmental decision making procedures, and the associated right to access to justice to claim for the realization of these rights.

[17] Very relevant for this point is the literature on environmental justice, which explicitly combines environmental protection and civil rights movements with the aim of eliminating the 'inequitable distribution of the burdens and benefits of environmental protection'. See Mutz, Bryner, and Kenney (2002: xxxi).

The absence of guaranteed freedom of thought and speech, the lack of a functioning and incorruptible judiciary, the inaccessibility of environment-related information, the absence of political freedoms and rights of association jeopardize activism, and imperil the creation of organizations, parties, and grassroots movements aimed at requesting the cessation of hazardous activities, changes in environmental law, the establishment of protected areas, and the like.

The most innovative pathway for the harmonization of human rights and environmental protection is the concept of environmental human rights. First introduced at the international level by Principle 1 of the 1972 Stockholm Declaration,[18] environmental human rights are recognized in the constitutions of 92 countries in different forms, such as the right to a non-hazardous environment (Switzerland), the right to live in a healthy environment (in almost all Latin American countries),[19] or the right to clean water (South Africa).[20] At the international level they are considered rights *de iure condendo* (proposals for the modification of existing law) by some

---

[18] Principle 1 of the Stockholm Declaration: 'Man has the fundamental right to freedom, equality and adequate conditions of life, in an environment of a quality that permits a life of dignity and well-being, and he bears a solemn responsibility to protect and improve the environment for present and future generations.'

[19] See Chapter 3 in Boyd (2012).

[20] See Chapter 3 in Boyd (2012). Today, out of 193 constitutions in the world, 147 include environmental provisions. Some have rudimentary references to the protection of national beauties and artistic heritage (such as Italy, Malta, Guatemala, and San Marino) while others include specific obligations of the government in protecting biodiversity, promotion of sustainable development for present and future generations (Sweden), prevention of pollution, or creation and preservation of protected areas (Portugal), and 83 include previsions concerning duties of citizens towards the conservation of the environment. See note 58 in Boyd (2012).

authors (Bosselmann 2015: 533),[21] while for others they are as yet too undetermined to become enforceable rights in international law in the near future (Lewis 2012a; Taylor 2008: 98). Though rapidly diffusing, the enforcement of environmental rights faces many difficulties, for example, concerning the delimitation of their scope, the parties involved, the possible claimants and plaintiffs, the fairness of the remedies, the proper role of courts, and the very content of environmental rights (May and Daly 2011).

Even if further clarified and recognized in international law, greened human rights, environmental procedural rights, and environmental human rights can be a support to conservation of the environment, but they remain limited in effectiveness. Human rights rhetoric is centred on the protection of human interests, which, therefore, cannot encompass environmental problems in their entirety. Neither can they grant environmental issues an indispensable priority in some cases, because human rights are based on a hierarchy at the top of which there are human beings (Taylor 2008: 98). Consequently, environmental human rights are not accompanied by an equally diffuse obligation on states, corporations, and individuals to protect the environment as a whole in order to fulfil such emerging human rights. Damages to the environment perpetuated by states, corporations, and individuals are taken into consideration only when they directly harm human rights, otherwise the protection of the environment does not figure as a human rights concern (Bosselmann 2015: 533–4). Moreover, the lack of centrality of the collective interests of society and the predominance of issues concerning 'classic' individual human rights—such as the right to health and life—remain 'ill-suited to addressing environmental degradation as such' (Francioni 2010: 44).[22]

---

[21] Bosselmann actually refers to a right as a *status nascendi* (emerging).

[22] Regional human rights courts are increasingly recognizing the detrimental effect of environmental damages on human rights but they struggle to give due consideration to collective claims; Grant (2015). The European

Rights to the environment remain linked to classical human rights theory, maintaining the strength of its rhetoric and its diffuse legal recognition, but staying concentrated on its core matter: humans. The foundations of human rights, and their inherent justification, are intrinsically anthropocentric as they aim at protecting fundamental human interests (Lewis 2012a: 45). Hence, the environment is perceived as having instrumental value, to be protected as long as it is relevant for the protection of human beings (Taylor 2008: 89). Human rights rhetoric and law are concerned with human subjects 'rather than from being anything else: not an animal, or a fish for example, and certainly not a tree or a habitat or a lake, no matter how magnificent' (Gearty 2010: 7; brackets omitted).[23]

Court of Human Rights recognizes the interconnectedness of a wide range of human rights—in particular, the right to private and family life—and environmental protection. However, it only accepts the claims of individual victims, thus limiting the standing to cases concerning harm to specific individual rights (Grant 2015: 161, 174). The Inter-American Court of Human Rights accepts claims brought by relatives and organizations of the victims, thereby facilitating the protection of a broader set of subjects. It has, for example, ruled on those indigenous peoples and local communities negatively affected by environmental harm. However, the Court has not yet gone beyond indigenous peoples and local communities as relevant collective entities in cases concerning environmental protection (Grant 2015: 165–7). Thus far, the institutions which are most able to respond to such claims seem to be the African Court and Commission on Human and Peoples' Rights, whose charter goes beyond the *greened* human rights, recognizing to all peoples the right to a satisfactory environment (Grant 2015: 167–73), Article 24. Moreover, admitting the standing of non-victims and public interest claims, the African system potentially includes claims against states for the protection of a general interest in conservation of the environment, rather than solely to end existing human rights violations.

[23] Different, and not falling within the realm of human rights rhetoric and law, is the idea of nature's rights. The Ecuadorian Constitution of 2008,

Mutually Harming?

Unfortunately, 'environmentalists and human rights advocates have seldom been the cosiest bed-fellows' (Rajan 2011: 106), and many have in fact wondered whether 'human rights help or hinder the environment' and vice versa (Gearty 2010). People need to use natural resources to survive, develop, and prosper at very different levels. Local and rural communities require access to the local environment to respond to their immediate necessities, states must use natural resources to (hopefully) respond to the needs of their populations. The urge to respond to human rights may even be used as an excuse to undertake activities that have a detrimental effect on the environment (Gearty 2010: 9), and poverty alleviation, if undertaken without an environmentally sustainable approach, is at risk of taxing 'biodiversity to death' (Sanderson and Redford 2003).

At the same time, 'for just as the human rights protagonist has often given the impression that he or she does not care about the natural world, so too have some environmentalists seemed at time to despise people' (Gearty 2010: 21)[24] and to value birds more than humans

---

which was followed by the Bolivian Constitution in 2009, was the first to ever recognize a set of rights to the environment: rights to existence, conservation, regeneration of life cycles, structure and function, and evolutionary processes (Article 71), and to bind the state to promote the protection and respect of natural assets. Recognizing nature as a right holder means to treat it as a subject, as a person. This presupposition—made explicit in Article 10—elevates nature to the level of humans and groups. The allocation of rights to nature in the Ecuadorian Constitution, therefore, follows a non-anthropocentric cosmocentric conception of the environment, such as those of indigenous peoples and Leopold, which presents the environment as a source of duties and responsibilities in its integrity, and where duties are concentrated on the actions that humans have to follow.

[24] See also Alcorn (2008).

(Diamond 2005: 441). Of course it depends on the type of activity pursued. For example, the reduction of pollution is hardly conceivable as a potential harm to human rights, although it may clash with the right to work if it requires the closing down of certain industries. Conservation science actions, instead, addressed more widely at protecting and restoring the diversity of life on earth may be particularly problematic,[25] especially for indigenous peoples and local communities. A brief look at the history of conservation practices is sufficient to realize how dangerously close to colonialism and imperialism it can be, and how embedded in the North–South divide its developments are.[26] The burden to reduce human impact on earth is principally borne by developing countries—most often ex-colonies of European empires—whose natural resources are richer, but whose economic possibilities are limited and human rights violation are higher.

[25] Conservation science, or conservation biology, is defined by the Society of Conservation Science as a mission-oriented discipline 'that focuses on how to protect and restore biodiversity, or the diversity of life on Earth'. In order to achieve its goal, the discipline focuses on heterogeneous objectives—'how is the diversity of life distributed around the planet? What threats does this diversity face? What can people do to reduce or eliminate these threats and, when possible, restore biological diversity and ecosystem health?'—and ranges between many scientific fields, including conservation biology, zoology, genetics, ecology, anthropology, economics, sociology, psychology, religions, and environmental ethics (Society for Conservation Biology 2017).

[26] The North–South divide describes the still-existing differences between richer countries and poorer countries, which mostly reflect the division between northern and southern countries. Although Australia and New Zealand are clear exceptions to a literal understanding of this label, the term 'North–South divide' is commonly used as an equivalent of developed and developing countries which, having a geographical focus, suggests fewer implications on whether certain countries are actually 'developing' or not, as well as on whether 'development' has only positive connotations.

The impulse to promote conservation actions in developing countries originated in the nineteenth and twentieth centuries from colonial authorities, who—influenced by 'local classifications and interpretations of the natural world and its symbols' and by a 'highly heterogeneous mixture of indigenous, Romantic, Orientalist and other elements' (Grove 1995: 3, 12)—started to sense the detrimental consequences of the environmental exploitation they themselves had been pursuing (Adams and Milligan 2003: 5). Their reaction positioned the environment between extensive exploitation for the sake of colonial interests on the one hand, and pristine[27] conservation, aimed at the preservation of wilderness at the expense of local people, on the other. The local relationships with the environment were depicted in racist and discriminatory ways, condemning the allegedly barbarous overuse of natural resources. The alternative model proposed by colonialists encompassed hunting areas accessible for the white elite only (Adams and Milligan 2003: 9),[28]

---

[27] The meaning of the term 'pristine' is quite controversial. It usually refers to ecosystems untouched by human activities, as opposed to human-influenced ones. This romantic dichotomy has been contested by indigenous peoples, anthropologists, archaeologists, and historical ecologists because many landscapes once considered 'pristine' are the result of the interactions between humans and nature; see Claus, Kai, and Satterfield (2010: 266). According to many authors, human beings have modified so many ecosystems since their appearance on the earth that it is impossible and pointless to distinguish between real and apparent *pristine* ecosystems; see Posey (1999b: 7); Agrawal and Gibson (1999: 632).

[28] See also MacKenzie (1988), who describes the evolution of hunting practices and laws in Africa and India in the nineteenth and early-twentieth century and their link to conservation. While indigenous peoples were prohibited from hunting for food and commerce, white colonizers developed hunting activities in areas subtracted and fenced off to local peoples. These areas were often later transformed—once deprived of their traditional occupiers and with decimated animal populations—into modern protected areas.

forests withdrawn from local use for future timber exploitation (Adams 2003: 26), and protected areas, these also accessible to white residents and visitors only.[29]

Since the creation of the first national park, the Yellowstone National Park in Montana in 1872,[30] conservation of the environment—of *wilderness*—in protected areas was institutionalized as being, by definition, separated from human life. People were fenced out and kept away from protected areas and natural resources (Morel 2010: 174), regardless of their needs and of their actual environmental impact. They were perceived as a threat to conservation (Claus, Kai, and Satterfield 2010: 268), and their interests as necessarily conflicting with those of ecosystems. Colonial science described local uses of natural resources as short-sighted and doomed to degrade ecosystems (Adams 2003: 30), hence peoples and communities present in protected areas were a threat to conservation objectives: 'the idea of nature as wilderness made hunters into poachers, wood-cutters into law-breakers, and farmers into the enemies of conservation' (Adams 2003: 35).[31] The vast use of land for the creation of national parks

[29] Adams (2003: 38) quotes a very interesting passage by the Irish physician and naturalist Richard Hingston (1931: 404), who describes the mentality still present in colonies in the first half of the twentieth century: 'What the sportsman wants is a good trophy, almost invariably a male trophy, and the getting of that usually satisfies him.... The position is not the same with the native hunter. He cares nothing about species or trophies or sex, nor does he hunt for the fun of the thing.'

[30] The Yellowstone National Park provides one of the most famous examples of 'fortress conservation'. It was established on indigenous territories, inhabited by Crow, Blackfeet, and Shoshone-Bannock peoples, causing the eviction of seven tribes that fought with park managers for 30 years, with a cost in terms of lives of about 300 people; see Daniels (2007: 552); Sobrevila (2008).

[31] See also Jacoby (2001).

in America, Australia, and Asia was in fact made possible by the forced removal or decimation of indigenous peoples (Claus, Kai, and Satterfield 2010: 263),[32] causing a great variety of violations of civil, economic, and cultural rights (Brechin et al. 2002: 45; UNGA 2016), such as: displacing communities from their lands, reducing or prohibiting access to natural resources important for essential services (livelihoods, housing, building materials, water sources), prohibiting access to culturally or spiritually significant areas and resources, denying self-determination, or refusing to abide by free prior informed consent (Campese 2009: 7; Jonas, Makagon, and Roe 2016: 18–25). This approach to conservation—which is not, regrettably, a relic of the past—has been named fortress conservation (Maffi 2014: 4) (or, also Yellowstone model, authoritarian protectionism, fences and fines approach) (Brechin et al. 2002; Sobrevila 2008: 7) and has created thousands of conservation refugees, mostly indigenous peoples.

Fortress conservation approaches have found a more recent and apparently less racist support—still at the expense of indigenous peoples—in the theory of the famous 'tragedy of the commons' formulated by Garrett Hardin (1968).[33] Hardin, searching for

[32] In a recent report of the Special Rapporteur of the Human Rights Council on the Rights of Indigenous Peoples, Victoria Tauli-Corpuz, it was calculated that up to 50 per cent of existing protected areas were created on lands and territories traditionally held by indigenous peoples; see UNGA (2016).

[33] Even though the legal and cultural systems of indigenous peoples and local communities are very diverse, it is possible to affirm that many manage lands and resources through a system of rules that can be described as a system of commons in which property is not 'centred on an individual but rather on the group and its community'; see Jaksa (2006: 186); Posey and Dutfield (1996). For an interesting reconstruction of the negative impact of the enclosure of the commons on indigenous peoples and local communities, see Chandra (2016b: 62–7).

the human factors negatively affecting the conservation of natural resources, reached two conclusions: the earth cannot sustain an indefinite growth of the human population, and the allocation and use of resources must be regulated either by a centralized government or by a system of private property.[34] 'Ruin is the destination towards which all men rush, each pursuing his own best interest in a society that believes in the freedom of the commons,' he writes in his famous article (Hardin 1968: 1244). Indigenous peoples and local communities, associated with the use of resources in commons, were hence described as threats to ecosystems because they inevitably would use them unsustainably (Becker and Ostrom 1995). The solutions suggested consisted of transforming commons into private property or state-controlled systems, such as privately owned conserved areas or governmental protected areas (Bavikatte 2014: 10).

Ironically, before the middle of the twentieth century, the organization of indigenous lands under systems of common property resulted in the same outcome for opposite reasons. Before being considered as barbarous and detrimental for conservation, and hence expelled from protected lands, indigenous peoples were considered savages who were 'part of nature' (Adams 2003: 35) and their organization in commons was used as an excuse to deny them any property rights over their lands (Banner 2005). Since they held lands in commons, without a system of private property and since most of them did not practise agriculture, their impact on the natural environment was not visible: no fences, no farmed fields. It was hence established that they owned no land

---

[34] Using a game theory approach, Hardin describes what he thinks would be the behaviour of a group of herdsmen sharing a grazing land, in common, in the absence of any restriction. According to Hardin, each herdsman would increase the number of his animals in order to increase his profits. Given that all herdsmen would act in the same way, the land would soon be so overgrazed that all herdsmen would lose all their animals.

(Jaksa 2006: 168), and the 'newly discovered' lands and resources could be used, and overused, by the colonizers. Paradoxically, precisely because of their low impact on the environment, indigenous peoples were not recognized as having any rights over their lands and were evicted with neither consent nor compensation (Manus 2005: 555)—while later, or on other occasions, they received the same treatment for opposite reasons.

Environmental Allies: Indigenous Peoples and Local Communities

Biocultural Diversity and Conservation

In the 1970s, the fortress conservation approach began to be questioned. This change of perspective was driven by the understanding of its frequent ineffectiveness, an increased recognition of the needs of developing countries, and a stronger perception and international recognition of the rights of indigenous peoples (Berkes 2004: 622; Meine 2010: 13). Policymakers, conservationists, and non-governmental organizations began to pay more attention to peoples and communities and began to develop rights-based or community-based conservation projects (Agrawal and Gibson 1999; Gavin et al. 2005; Reed 2008: 2420). It was also recognized that conservation without community involvement can be less effective or even detrimental for biodiversity conservation (Oudenhoven, Mijatovic, and Eyzaguirre 2010: 8) because indigenous peoples and local communities 'serve numerous and important roles in protecting and maintaining natural areas' (Schmidt and Peterson 2000: 1459), holding important traditional knowledge about the local environment and having institutions, customary laws, and ethical systems which reflect local ecological contexts. Moreover, conservation programmes that disregard the rights of indigenous peoples and local communities bear the cost of displacement, compensation (when it can be afforded), and creation of alternative livelihoods, and are harder to enforce due to conflicts with the affected communities (Agrawal and Gibson 1999).

Furthermore, in the late 1980s, studies by Elinor Ostrom, winner of the Nobel Prize, challenged the theory of the tragedy of the commons (Becker and Ostrom 1995; Ostrom 1990) and proved that communities, under certain conditions, can be more effective in the sustainable long-term use of natural resources than state-controlled or private property systems (Nonini 2007; Ostrom 1990: 1). It is important to note that the commons-like system that Ostrom describes is not a system without rules or institutions. It is not a state of freedom and lack of coercion, as the herdsmen system pictured by Hardin. Ostrom's system of commons is a system that presents a combination of clearly defined boundaries, rules that are adapted to local conditions and that allocate resources to users, participation of most resource users in decision-making processes, effective control of compliance to rules by subjects accountable to the users, graduated sanctions for users that do not comply with rules, local and low-cost conflict-resolutions mechanisms, self-determination of users, and long-term tenure rights over resources (Becker and Ostrom 1995: 119). Property systems of indigenous peoples and local communities, if they have a certain level of self-determination and long-term tenure rights over their lands and resources, resemble Ostrom's commons. Their commons are often ruled by customary laws that grant rights to and impose obligations on members, have institutions which coordinate behaviours and monitor compliance with rules, and are usually 'small enough' to make each person's action noticeable to the others, thereby limiting free-riding.[35] Hence, if they have certain fundamental rights to self-determination and rights over lands and resources they can be in a position to actually promote the conservation of the local environment.

The idea of the existence of a long-term, sustainable, and mutually beneficial relationship between certain communities and peoples and the environment was framed by Darrel Posey (1999a) using the term

---

[35] A free-rider is a person that benefits from a good or service without bearing the costs of its creation and conservation; see Olson (1965).

'biocultural diversity'.[36] This term refers to the existence of an 'inextricable link' (Maffi 2007: 267) between cultural and biological diversity, which denotes 'the idea that maintaining and restoring the diversity of life means sustaining both biodiversity and cultures, because the two are interrelated and mutually supportive' (Maffi and Woodley 2010: 1). Biocultural diversity of indigenous peoples and local communities includes vast knowledge about the ecosystems of their lands and their biotic and abiotic elements;[37] centrality of the environment in their practices and beliefs (Slikkerveer 1999); social, cultural (Dutfield 1999: 550),[38] spiritual, economic, and political practices shaped around the ecological elements of the territories where they reside, their nomadic routes, and their sacred sites (Kothari et al. 2012: 19). Ethnobiological and ethnoecological research has provided evidence of the contribution of indigenous peoples and local communities to the conservation of biodiversity by safeguarding their very diverse ecosystems, using species sustainably, practising techniques that maintain an equilibrium among species, and selecting new varieties of domestic plants and animals (Bèlair et al. 2010: 9; Valderrama and Arico 2010).[39]

[36] For a brief history of the use of the term 'biocultural diversity', see K. Wilson (2016).

[37] The relevance of abiotic elements might be underestimated by the use of the term *bio*cultural. For this reason, some have proposed the use of the term *eco*cultural diversity; see Jonas, Makagon, and Shrumm (2013, n. 3). In this book, the term 'biocultural diversity' is preferred in order to remain consistent with most literature on the topic.

[38] Particular attention has been given to the correlation between linguistic diversity and biological diversity—because of reflections of environmental features in local languages, because of the their common areas of distribution, and because of common threats to their conservation; see Maffi (2005: 600).

[39] It is estimated that indigenous peoples' territories today cover about 22 per cent of the planet and that within these territories 80 per cent of total

Indigenous peoples and local communities that lived and continue to live away from mainstream societies and their markets and cities 'know their lives and immediate futures—as well as the well-being of future generations—depend upon the environments in which they live and the biodiversity upon which they depend' (Maffi 2014: 4).[40] They directly rely on local ecosystem services for their livelihoods, building materials and medicines, and their cultural and spiritual practices are built around natural sites, plants, animals, rivers, streams, and shores. Hence, they know that the degradation of their surrounding ecosystems and the loss of biodiversity would profoundly threaten their survival and culture (Posey 1999b: 7). Instead, in industrial societies, people obtain their livelihoods from many different sources distributed around the world, and disperse their wastes away from their lands. Therefore, the overexploitation and destruction of one resource or ecosystem does not appear significant, because 'they turn to another' (Cocks 2006: 188) and easily 'forget that as biological beings [they] are as dependent on clean air and water, uncontaminated soil and biodiversity as any other creature' (Suzuki 1999: 72).

Interestingly, many studies show different, but similar, relationships of care between indigenous peoples and local communities, and the environment (Cocks 2006: 188). One of the first comprehensive books on the topic was edited by Posey (1999a). It is a collection of studies from different parts of the world that highlights the importance given by the spiritual and cultural values of indigenous and local communities to the conservation of biodiversity. More recently, the action-research project by the International Institute for Environment and Development, *Protecting Community Rights over Traditional Knowledge* (Swiderska et al. 2009), describes common customary

---

biodiversity is held; see Sobrevila (2008). This estimate does not include the territories occupied and managed by local communities because of lack of data.

[40] See also Maffi and Woodley (2010: 4).

values and world views in five indigenous communities in Kenya, Peru, Panama, and India. The communities, involved in a project aimed at finding sui generis instruments to protect traditional knowledge,[41] have all shown to share holistic world views based on the assumption that everything in nature is interconnected and interdependent: humans, as well as traditional knowledge, practices, and customary laws, are elements of nature. In their world view, everything in nature is worthy of respect and the exploitation of natural resources is regulated by customary laws whose enforcement is supervised by spirits or gods.[42] Similarly, a study by the Forest Peoples Programme (2011) documented the sustainability of the use of natural resources by indigenous communities in Suriname, Cameroon, Guyana, Thailand,

---

[41] Together with traditional lands and territories, traditional knowledge is considered the foundation of indigenous cultures; see UN Permanent Forum on Indigenous Issue (2004). Tobin (2009) argues that indigenous rights to life, health, food, and culture depend on the maintenance and development of such knowledge as a dynamic element that emanates from the connection with the natural world and that is collectively held and shared among communities and peoples. Throughout the world, traditional knowledge is widely accessed during research for non-commercial purposes and for research on the development of new commercial products in pharmaceutical, cosmetic, food, and other industries; see Ten Kate and Laird (1999); Laird and Wynberg (2008). Many are the examples of acts of so-called 'biopiracy', which see international corporations accessing traditional knowledge associated with biological resources without the people's/community's consent and remaining the only beneficiaries of sometimes enormous profits; see Mgbeoji (2006).

[42] Studies have also revealed that the communities are guided by common ethical principles: reciprocity in exchanges with nature (as much that is taken is given back); equilibrium with nature (society must be in harmony with nature); and duality within nature (everything has a complementary opposite and balance must be kept); see Swiderska et al. (2009).

and Bangladesh. The study shows that traditional knowledge and customary law systems of communities guide the wise use of local resources under the idea of a spiritual connection with the lands. Further evidence has been provided by an extensive study organized by the IUCN and other supporting organizations on sacred natural sites (Verschuuren et al. 2010).[43] The study provides evidence of the relevance of sacred natural sites, mostly attributed to indigenous and local communities, for biodiversity and the conservation of ecosystems. A literature review of a hundred different studies from Africa and Asia has shown that sacred meanings attributed either to nature itself or to heroes, structures, or histories connected to the territory, have led to the preservation of reservoirs of biodiversity equally rich, or richer, than protected areas close by.

When 'combined with effective local governance and conservation of nature', territories and areas of indigenous peoples and local communities have recently been characterised by the term Indigenous Peoples and Local Communities' Conserved Territories and Areas (ICCAs). ICCAs are defined as the 'natural and/or modified ecosystems containing significant biodiversity values, ecological services and cultural values, conserved by indigenous peoples and local communities, both sedentary and mobile, through customary laws or other effective means' (Kothari et al. 2012: 6). They are described as those areas and territories to which a 'well-defined people or community possesses a close and profound relation'; where 'the people or community is the primary player in decision-making and implementation regarding the management'; and where 'the people's or community's management decision and efforts lead to the conservation of habitats, species, genetic diversity, ecological processes, and associated

---

[43] In the study, sacred natural sites are defined as 'areas of lands or water having special spiritual significance to peoples and communities' (Verschuuren et al.: 1).

cultural values, whether or not the conscious objective of management is conservation *per se'* (Jonas et al. 2012: 6). Interestingly, ICCAs diverge from the protected area model because they do not rest on centralized top–down management, whose objective is precisely, and centrally, the conservation of the environment of a certain territory, but rather they are the product of heterogeneous ways of life, knowledge systems, and world views which result in effective conservation, which is not imposed by external authorities.[44]

These recent understandings have led many to redefine environmental conservation in a more 'social fashion' (Brosius and Russell 2003: 55, cited in Berkes (2004)) with the aim to, besides ecological goals, embrace social and political elements (such as, human dignity, legitimacy, governance, accountability, adaptation and learning, and non-local forces) (Brechin et al. 2002: 43–4) and to balance conservation goals with respect towards the rights of indigenous peoples and local communities (Brechin et al.). Today, many international organizations working on conservation issues, such as the IUCN, WWF, Conservation International, United Nations Environment Programme (UNEP), and Nature Conservancy, recognize the role of indigenous peoples in the conservation of biodiversity (Schmidt and Peterson 2009: 1459; Maffi 2014: 4). In particular, the IUCN has played a central role in promoting new ways to manage protected areas that involve, rather than exclude, local communities. The IUCN World Conservation Congress has passed several resolutions on indigenous peoples on issues such as protected areas, traditional biodiversity knowledge, forests, marine and coastal areas, and mining (Roe et al. 2010). The recently adopted IUCN Programme 2017–2020 reaffirms

---

[44] ICCAs are increasingly recognized worldwide—see the work of the ICCA Consortium (www.iccaconsortium.org)—nevertheless, they are still under threat from industrial activities and environmental degradation, and their holders still lack effective recognition of the rights necessary to maintain their role as conservation stewards (Jonas et al. 2012: 5).

the principle that conservation and human progress are understood as mutually supportive and includes among the aims of the organization the increased protection of rights of indigenous peoples (IUCN 2016).

As the Special Rapporteur of the Human Rights Council on the Rights of Indigenous Peoples has recently reported to the UNGA, the evolution of conservation techniques towards rights-based approaches has decreased violations of rights of indigenous peoples and local communities, but 'significant gaps remain between these policies and their effective implementation on the ground' (UNGA 2016). Although evictions of indigenous peoples for conservation purposes still occur on a daily basis, and many still question the effectiveness of rights-based approaches, it is true that indigenous peoples have, at least in the theory and rhetoric of conservation, started to move from the role of the victims to the role of potential allies: 'the idea of indigeneity that has now captured public attention conceives of such peoples as the original trustees of the earth' (Bavikatte and Bennett 2015: 18).

From Myth to Reality

> Some of the indigenous peoples and the anthropologists ... insist that past indigenous peoples were (and modern ones still are) gentle and ecologically wise stewards of their environments, intimately knew and respected Nature, innocently lived in a virtual Garden of Eden, and could never have done all those bad things.... Only those evil modern First World inhabitants are ignorant of Nature, don't respect the environment, and destroy it. (Diamond 2005: 9)

Assumptions about the correlation of indigenous peoples and biological diversity immediately recall the famous myth of the 'noble savage', and in particular that of the ecologically noble savage, which describes indigenous peoples as pacifist friends of nature, too good, and too primitive, to harm the environment. Considering the popularity of the myth, it is important to clarify its meaning and scope and, most importantly, to distance oneself from it.

The term 'noble savage', commonly understood as 'a mythic personification of natural goodness by a romantic glorification of savage life', was first used by Marc Lescarbot in his book *Histoire de la Nouvelle-France*, in 1609 (Ellingson 2001: 1, xv). It is usually attributed to Jean-Jacques Rousseau, and in particular, to his book *Discours sur l'origine et les fondements de l'inégalité parmi les hommes* (*Discourse on the Origin and Basis of Inequality Among Mankind*), although Rousseau never actually used the expression *bon sauvage*. Two hundred years later, John Crawfurd, the president of the Ethnological Society of London, in his article 'On the Conditions which Favour, Retard or Obstruct the Early Civilization of Man', used the term 'noble savage' with a clear racist, anti–human rights intent. In the article, where *race* is considered the first and most significant factor for the civilization of a people, the two parts of the term are disentangled and 'savage' is deprived of any form of nobility: 'I cannot ... conceive anything noble in the poor naked, crouching creature, trembling with cold and starving from hunger.' (Crawfurd 1861: 159)

Today the myth of the noble savage is still debated by scholars of different fields—anthropologists, conservationists, ethnobiologists, geographers—and in 1990, the publication by the conservationist Kent Redford titled, 'The Ecologically Noble Savage', granted the myth a new and slightly different 'resurrection' (Ellingson 2001: 344). This time, the 'nobleness' was modernized by describing it as 'ecological,' but criticized as well. In his brief but incisive article, Redford (1991: 47) argues that 'there is no cultural barrier to the Indians' adoption of means to "improve" their lives (i.e., make them more like Western lives), even if the long-term sustainability of the resource base is threatened'. Redford underlines that indigenous peoples (and local communities) have the same capacities, desires, and needs as Western people. Therefore, to assume that 'when confronted with market pressures, higher population densities, and increased sedentism most indigenous peoples will maintain the integrity of their traditional methods', is to fall into the 'ideological trap' of the myth of the ecologically noble savage.[45] The myth suggests that all indigenous peoples have had— and have preserved—sustainable lifestyles, just as if they had some inherent features that define their sustainable relationship with the environment and that run so deeply that they are independent from external conditions (an idea that somehow dangerously links nobility to hypothetical 'savage genes' and 'indigenous races').[46]

Even though the research in this book is based on the idea of indigenous peoples living sustainably, it rests on the understanding that there is no benefit in romanticizing them—not even those living sustainably (Posey 1999b: 7). To point out the dangers of the noble savage myth is not to claim that indigenous peoples and local communities do not have cultural, spiritual, and legal systems that guide their relationships with the environment towards sustainable paths. It is simply to acknowledge that not all indigenous peoples and local communities have preserved sustainable practices and world views and that once sustainable practices may become unsustainable when changes—such as population density, abundance of land, involvement in a market economy—occur. The noble savage myth gives too simplistic a representation of reality (Claus, Kai, and Satterfield 2010: 269). The denial of the variability of internal and external conditions

[45] Assumptions about indigenous eco-responsibility have recently been further questioned by archaeological discoveries that seem to have revealed that during the post-Pleistocene era—before the arrival of the European invasion—destruction of habitats and extinction of species has occurred around the world, see Terborgh (2000: 1358). See also the section titled 'Facing Responsibilities' in Chapter 1 of this book.

[46] In this book, it would be neither adequate nor helpful to dwell on the critics of classical racism. But it is important to underline that the theory embraced here is that of geneticists Luigi Cavalli-Sforza and Guido Barbujani who scientifically reject the notion of existence of human races; see Cavalli-Sforza, Menozzi, and Piazza (2004); Barbujani (2004).

endangers collaboration between indigenous peoples, local communities, and conservation practitioners, and 'resurgent protectionist arguments' are a threatening consequence, which is both 'operationally unrealistic and morally questionable' (Wilshusen 2002: 18).

New versions of fortress conservation are being proposed, with returns to the same mistakes of the past ('tantamount to reinventing a square wheel') (Wilshusen 2002), precisely because a too 'black and white' description of conservation realities has sometimes been provided (Lu Holt 2005: 204). If indigenous peoples and local communities are described as either traditional noble savages, who are 'natural conservationists', or peoples corrupted by development and detrimental for the environment (Terborgh 2000: 1359), no space is left for adaptation, resilience, and for the paramount importance of local institutions, and the only option left seems to be the creation of protected areas (Wilshusen 2002: 32). 'Locals are caught in a conservation Catch-22' if the introduction of new economic activities or technologies—often adopted for survival—doom them to lose their 'pristine noble savageness' and, with it, their conservationist label (Lu Holt 2005: 209).[47] This protectionist turn is fuelled by imaginary descriptions of noble savages and by the denial of indigenous peoples' and local communities' agency to determine changes while remaining sustainable. Most importantly, this turn alienates potential allies and ignores that 'nature protection can and should occur in ways that are not just ecologically sound but also pragmatically feasible and socially just' (Wilshusen et al. 2002: 18, 36). On the contrary, the recognition of the potential role of certain indigenous peoples and local communities

[47] A Catch-22—an expression first used in Joseph Heller's satirical novel *Catch-22* about bureaucratic loopholes in wartime—is 'an impossible situation where you are prevented from doing one thing until you have done another thing that you cannot do until you have done the first thing'; see Cambridge University Press (2017).

as conservation allies can be, if cleared from the naivety and dangers of the noble savage myth, a route for the protection of the environment in ways that respect and promote human rights.

The equilibrium between protecting the environment and enforcing human rights remains an uneasy one. But denying the help of such conservation allies means to surrender to a zero-sum game, where either the environment or human rights of indigenous peoples and local communities are inevitably violated. Biocultural rights were conceived by Bavikatte (2014: 18) precisely as a 'people-led alternative to state-led technocratic solutions to the environmental crisis'.

4   Of Rights and Responsibilities

Getting to Know Biocultural Rights

What Are They?

As seen in Chapter 3, human rights and conservation of the environment have a peculiar relationship. It was noted how human rights to the environment, though important to protect very fundamental human interests, appear too limited to sufficiently tackle the current environmental crisis because they retain, as human rights, a fully anthropocentric approach. Meanwhile, conservation science actions aimed at protecting the environment bear the legacy of a colonial past, and are in danger of harming the rights of indigenous peoples and local communities when trapped in 'state-led technocratic solutions' (Bavikatte 2014: 18). The recognition of the role of indigenous peoples and local communities as stewards of the environment clears the way for new solutions which are gaining recognition among conservation practitioners and international law. According to Sanjay Bavikatte, this recognition is taking the shape of a new set of emerging rights, biocultural rights.

The concept of biocultural rights was first proposed by Bavikatte in 2010.[1] Drawing on the wording of the CBD and its Nagoya Protocol, and on other environment-related UN treaties and declarations,[2] Bavikatte (2014: 1) argues that biocultural rights are a new set of third-generation rights in the process of being recognized. He traces their origin to the convergence of the post-development movement, the commons movement, and the movement for the recognition of the rights of indigenous peoples and local communities (Bavikatte 2014: 16), charting their development in 'multilateral environmental agreements, domestic legislation, case law, shifts in development discourse and the struggles of communities' (Bavikatte 2014: 2). As indigenous peoples and local communities 'highlight their role as guardians of ecosystems and the significance of their cultural and spiritual bonds with Nature' (Bavikatte 2014: 16), international environmental law, he explains, increasingly acknowledged the relevance

[1] Bavikatte's is an intense and thoughtfully researched book, which covers issues ranging from economics, law, and anthropology to philosophy. He covers extensively the concept of property, its origins, and development, the significance of the relationship between personhood, peoplehood, property, indigenous commons, and stewardship, and Anglo-American court cases relevant for biocultural rights jurisprudence.

This book only focuses on the interpretation of the concept of biocultural rights, and in no way expects to fully embrace the fascinating landscape pictured by Bavikatte.

[2] Among which are the UN Convention to Combat Desertification, UN Framework on Convention on Climate Change, UN Forum on Forests, Food and Agriculture Organization of the United Nations (FAO), and IUCN; see Bavikatte (2014: 16–20).

of traditional knowledge, practices, and ways of life of indigenous peoples and local communities for the conservation of the environment, and recognized their rights to 'fulfil their role as trustees of their cultures, lands, waters, and resources' (Bavikatte 2014: 21).

States are called to assume their responsibilities towards the environment not only through *fortress conservation* with the creation of protected areas, seed banks, and green technologies—which he labels state-led technocratic solutions—but also by respecting the rights of peoples and communities to participate in the management of their territories and to preserve and promote their traditional knowledge.[3] Biocultural rights 'denote all the rights required to secure the stewardship role of communities over their lands and waters' (Bavikatte 2014: 16), and build on values, world views, practices, knowledge, and institutions of indigenous peoples and local communities beneficial for the conservation of the environment. Bavikatte describes them as rights of communities 'that have historically cared for their ecosystems ... irrespective of whether or not they have a formal title to it' (Bavikatte 2014: 143). 'The demand for biocultural rights,' he underlines, 'does not take as its point of departure the inherent right of a group or community to flourish, but rather ... the ethic of stewardship: it is the ethic of stewardship and not the group *per se* that justifies the right' (Bavikatte 2014: 142–3).

In the biocultural rights discourse, the call of indigenous peoples and local communities for the recognition of rights over lands and natural resources is closely connected with the recognition of their role as 'conservationists' of local ecosystems (Bavikatte 2014: 21–7). Both claims are relevant at the global level but are rooted at the local level. Since the 1970s, indigenous peoples have engaged in a worldwide campaign for the recognition of their rights but, as their name

---

[3] Rio Declaration, Principle 22; Agenda 21, Sections 2.10 and 3.26; Nagoya Protocol, Articles 6.2, 7, 12.1, and 16.

suggests, it is a global campaign of local peoples. The global character of environmental issues originates from the late nineteenth century (Sands et al. 2012: 4), when states understood that pollution and other ecological disasters do not respect national boundaries. The two claims merged into one big stream when the environmental movement started to abandon fortress conservation approaches and indigenous peoples began to be considered as potential partners rather than opponents (Bavikatte and Robinson 2011: 50).[4] The idea of biocultural rights emerged as an alternative to traditional conservation approaches, as a means to achieve protection of the environment, not only to preserve 'unspoiled wilderness' (Bavikatte 2014: 6) through the exclusion of indigenous peoples and local communities, but also to preserve biocultural diversity, recognizing their right to exercise the stewardship of their territories.

Biocultural rights build on two convergent claims: one for the recognition of rights of indigenous peoples and local communities and the other for the ending of the unsustainable and destructive use of biodiversity. Accordingly, Bavikatte and Robinson (2011: 50) explain, while the concept of biocultural rights recalled the rhetoric of the right to self-determination, it focused on the protection of the environment by enhancing the link between communities and ecosystems.

Biocultural rights appear to be based on the following understanding: some indigenous peoples and local communities have maintained sustainable lifestyles which are relevant for the conservation of their ecosystems and for the promotion of the sustainable use of natural resources; these ways of life can survive and flourish only if certain group rights over lands, resources, culture, and customary law are secured to such peoples and communities; the recognition of this set of group rights can thus enable and enhance the conservation of

---

[4] See the subsection titled 'Biocultural Diversity and Conservation' in Chapter 3 of this book.

ecosystems and the sustainable use of natural resources (Bavikatte 2014: 112–15; Bavikatte and Robinson 2011: 50).

It is these three understandings that converge in the concept of bio-cultural rights as a 'basket' of rights (and, as will be discussed below, their inherent duties), promoting their two foundations: the promotion and conservation of the cultural identity and self-determination of indigenous peoples and local communities on the one side, and conservation of the environment on the other.

Emerging (Biocultural) Rights

In his book, Bavikatte aims at mapping the emergence and recognition of the 'tendency in environmental jurisprudence towards the affirmation of biocultural rights' (Bavikatte 2014: 2). He does not describe existing international law, either in the form of treaties, conventions, or non-binding declarations, or in the form of custom. However, Bavikatte's is not simply a speculative reflection about a supposed moral right stemming from his aspirations and hopes. The concept of biocultural rights is more than an *opinio de iure condendo*.[5] It is the result of legal argumentation which waves an imaginary wire that connects heterogeneous facts and words that have developed and are developing in the rhetoric, treaties, declarations, and court decisions concerning indigenous peoples and local communities and conservation of the environment. His voice is the voice of the doctrine, of a public law scholar who sees a coherent and rational, though implicit, design in international documents, and his hope is that by telling and retelling the *story* of biocultural rights, and through the elaboration of doctrines and theories, 'biocultural rights will come alive' (Bavikatte 2014: 115).

---

[5] See the section titled 'Human Rights from Scratch' in Chapter 2 of this book.

International Documents, Conventions, and Declarations

The increasing recognition of the link between indigenous peoples and local communities and the environment has influenced international political declarations and conventions and has led to the recognition of specific provisions and inclusion of references to communities and peoples in environment-focused documents (Manus 2005). Among them is the Brundtland report, *Our Common Future*, issued in 1987 by the UN World Commission on Environment and Development, which affirms that indigenous traditional knowledge and experience offer valuable lessons for the sustainable management of natural resources and ecosystems, and which calls for the recognition of rights to such communities as a means to maintain their traditional sustainable ways of life (World Commission on Environment and Development 1987).[6] Along the same lines, the Rio Declaration of 1992 acknowledges that 'indigenous people and their communities and other local communities have a vital role in environmental management and development because of their knowledge and traditional

---

[6] See chapter titled 'Our Common Future, From One Earth to One World', para 46, and chapter 4, para 74). The Brundtland Report states:

> The starting point for a just and humane policy for such groups is the recognition and protection of their traditional rights to land and the other resources that sustain their way of life—rights that may define in terms that do not fit into standard legal systems. These groups' own institutions to regulate rights and obligations are crucial for maintaining the harmony with nature and the environmental awareness characteristic of the traditional way of life. Hence the recognition of traditional rights must go hand in hand with measures to protect local institutions that enforce responsibility in resource use. And this recognition must also give local communities a decisive voice in the decisions about resource use in the area. (para 75)

practices.[7] Agenda 21, the voluntary plan of action developed at the Rio Summit, calls on states to fulfil their responsibility towards the environment, respecting the right of indigenous peoples to participate in the management of their territories and helping the preservation and promotion of their traditional knowledge.[8]

In 1993, the first binding international agreement recognizing the role of indigenous peoples and local communities for conservation, the CBD, entered into force. The CBD was welcomed as a great step forward by indigenous peoples' movements because, besides affirming the close dependency of indigenous peoples and local communities[9] on biological resources,[10] it explicitly recognizes the importance of their knowledge, innovations, and customary practices for the conservation and sustainable use of the environment in Articles 8j and 10c, and calls on states to protect and encourage the wider application of their customary use of biological resources as a means to achieve the conservation of biodiversity.

In 2010, after extensive negotiations, the parties to the CBD adopted the Nagoya Protocol on Access to Genetic Resources and the Fair and Equitable Sharing of Benefits Arising from their Utilization, which entered into force in 2014.[11] Its objective is the regulation of the access and use of genetic resources and traditional knowledge and

---

[7] Rio Declaration, Principle 22.

[8] In particular, Part III, chapter 26 of Agenda 21.

[9] The text of the CBD refers to 'indigenous and local communities' rather than to indigenous peoples. After years of advocacy by indigenous peoples' representatives, the XXII Conference of the Parties has agreed 'to use the terminology "indigenous peoples and local communities" in future decisions and secondary documents under the Convention'; see CBD (2014: 16).

[10] CBD, Preamble.

[11] For a detailed analysis of the Nagoya Protocol and its provisions, see Greiber et al. (2012); Morgera, Tsioumani, and Buck (2014).

the equitable and fair sharing of the benefits arising from their use—access and benefit sharing (ABS)—to contribute to the conservation of biodiversity and sustainable use of its components.[12] Bavikatte (2014: 26, 109) defines the Nagoya Protocol as a 'high profile victory for biocultural rights', as it is the product of years of struggle and fight of indigenous peoples' representatives and international organizations to achieve an international recognition of the role of indigenous peoples and local communities in conservation of the environment. According to the framework, indigenous peoples and local communities—'historically the main actors involved in saving seeds, cross-breeding, and developing techniques to conserve and sustain crop and plant varieties' (Chandra 2016b: 92)—are entitled to the fair and equal sharing of the benefits that arise from the use of their traditional knowledge and associated resources, to the right to prior informed consent, the right to negotiate mutually agreed terms and to the right to customary use and exchange of their genetic resources.

The Protocol builds on the principle of sovereignty of states over the genetic resources found in their territories[13] but limits their sovereignty by the recognition of specific rights to indigenous peoples and local communities. In the preamble, states agree to recognize the interrelationship between genetic resources and indigenous peoples' and local communities' traditional knowledge and sustainable livelihood.[14] Articles 5, 6, and 7 require states to ensure that genetic resources and traditional knowledge are accessed with the prior informed consent of the communities and peoples of origin and that the benefits arising

---

[12] Nagoya Protocol, Article 1.

[13] Preamble of the Nagoya Protocol. See also CBD, Article 3.

[14] The Nagoya Protocol is already influencing the making of national legislations in many developing countries and is thus contributing to the recognition of indigenous rights over traditional knowledge and, in some states, to the genetic resources found in their territories.

from their use are equally shared with them. Moreover, Articles 12 and 22 call on parties to implement their obligations under the Protocol taking into consideration indigenous and local communities' customary laws as well as their community protocols (documents in which they assert their rights, goals, and world views) when dealing with the access and use of natural resources and traditional knowledge.[15]

In 2004, under the umbrella of the FAO, the International Treaty on Plant Genetic Resources for Food and Agriculture (ITPGRFA) entered into force, recognizing what it calls a set of 'farmers' rights'. Farmers' rights are defined by the FAO (1989: Resolution 5/89, para 108) as 'rights arising from the past, present and future contributions of farmers in conserving, improving and making available plant genetic resources, particularly those in center of origin/diversity. The purpose of these rights is stated to be ensuring full benefits to farmers and supporting the continuation of their contributions'.

Article 9 recognizes the contribution that indigenous peoples and local communities and, more broadly, farmers have made towards the conservation and development of plant genetic diversity. It calls on states to promote, through yet unspecified national measures, the conservation of traditional knowledge and practices of farmers, to share the benefits arising from the use of farmers' plant genetic resources and to involve them in relevant decision-making procedures. The article is very specific and concerns only plant genetic resources, but it builds on the acknowledgement of the role of certain indigenous peoples and local communities in the conservation of natural resources and calls on states, although timidly, to promote such conservation through the recognition of rights.

---

[15] For an example and a more extensive explanation of what such community protocols are, see the section titled 'An Example: Learning from the Khwe' in Chapter 5 of this book.

The case of the UN Framework Convention on Climate Change (UNFCCC),[16] which entered into force in 1994, is different—it does not make a reference to indigenous peoples and local communities. Progress has been made in the Paris Agreement, which entered into force in 2016, which acknowledges that actions to address climate change should respect, promote, and consider obligations on the rights of indigenous peoples and local communities (Preamble), and that adaptation action 'should be based on and guided by the best available science and, as appropriate, traditional knowledge, knowledge of indigenous peoples and local knowledge systems' (Article 7). These provisions, although a step forward, remain particularly soft, non-specific, and non-binding (Ferraris and Traynor 2016: 8).

The debate on the Programme on Reducing Emissions from Deforestation and Forest Degradation (REDD), aimed at reducing the emission of carbon dioxide (CO_2) by compensating 'national governments and subnational actors in return for demonstrable reductions in carbon emissions from deforestation and forest degradation and enhancements of terrestrial carbon stocks', is more forward-looking (Agrawal, Nepstad, and Chhatre 2011: 374). After a first period of absence (Jodoin 2016: 166)—culminating in the 'No Rights, no REDD' outcry by the Indigenous Peoples caucus at the 14th Conference of the Parties of the UNFCCC—REDD became REDD+ (REDD and the role of conservation, sustainable management of forests, and enhancement of forest carbon stocks in developing countries) and timidly started to include references to the rights of indigenous peoples and local communities in the 2009

[16] The UN Convention on Combating Desertification (1994) does not make, as yet, an explicit reference to rights that may be framed as seeds of biocultural rights. However, it makes reference to indigenous peoples and local communities as subjects of special consideration and as subjects to be included in development programmes; see Ziegler et al. (2008).

Cancun Agreement. However, today, even though REDD+ has committed to foster the respect of the rights of indigenous peoples and forest-dependent communities, it is still object of fierce critiques from indigenous peoples and local communities.[17]

Court Cases and Laws

Before moving to the sections dedicated to the analysis of the construct of biocultural rights, it is interesting to look at the case of *Endorois Welfare Council* v. *Kenya*[18] of the African Commission on Human and People's Rights,[19] which Bavikatte mentions as evidence of the emergence of biocultural rights.[20] In *Endorois Welfare Council*,

---

[17] The focus on tenure rights and the lack of effective implementation and enforcement programmes aimed at specifically safeguarding the rights of indigenous peoples and local communities currently leaves them quite unprotected vis-à-vis violations of their rights. For more on the problems linked to the conception and implementation of REDD, see Agrawal, Nepstad, and Chhatre (2011: 379); Savaresi (2012); Godden and Tehan (2016).

[18] *Centre for Minority Rights Development (Kenya) and Minority Rights Group (on behalf of Endorois Welfare Council)* v. *Kenya*, African Commission on Human and Peoples' Rights, No. 276 (2003), (hereinafter referred to as *Endorois Welfare Council*).

[19] The African Commission on Human and Peoples' Rights is a quasi-judicial body that judges, together with the African Court (recently entrusted with judicial powers), on the African Charter on Human and Peoples' Rights. The Charter is one of the milestone binding agreements within the AU framework, which came into life in 2002, and acts through the determination of common policies for its member states.

[20] In Chapter 7 of his book, Bavikatte (2014) also analyses the cases of *Mayagna (Sumo) Awas Tingni Community* v. *Nicaragua*; *Moiwana Village* v. *Suriname*; and *Saramaka People* v. *Suriname*, decided by the Inter-American Court on Human Rights.

the African Commission adopted a decision in 2009, which was then approved by the African Union (AU) in 2010. In the decision, the Commission interpreted the African Charter as imposing on states the obligation to balance the value of conservation of the environment with the rights of indigenous peoples to culture, development, and access to natural resources, and the obligation to promote and conserve a healthy environment for the precise aim of respecting the rights of indigenous peoples.

The Endorois are an indigenous people of about 60,000 members, who have traditionally lived as pastoralists in the Rift Valley in Kenya (Bavikatte 2014: 160). In 1978, the Kenyan government declared the area as the Lake Bogoria Game Reserve and evicted the Endorois people without their consultation, but promising them compensation for displacement, the sharing of the revenues derived from management of the Reserve, and the distribution of new lands. By 2003, only very little monetary compensation had been received by a small part of the community and all other promises had not been met.

In that year, the Endorois presented their case at the African Commission, which ruled in their favour. The Commission recognized the Endorois to be indigenous peoples, who had communal property rights over their traditional lands because of their continued occupancy (until the forceful eviction) and because of their special religious and cultural relationship with the lands.[21] The Commission recognized that the relationship with the lands and their natural resources was paramount for their survival and identity and declared that only very exceptional public interests[22] could justify their eviction, even with compensation. Most interestingly, the Commission declared that in this case, the creation of a conservation area was a non-reasonable justification because 'the Endorois—as the ancestral guardians of that

---

[21] *Endorois Welfare Council*, paras 243–4.

[22] *Endorois Welfare Council*, para 212.

land—are best equipped to maintain its delicate ecosystems ... [and] the Endorois are prepared to continue the conservation work begun by the Government'.[23]

As Bavikatte (2014: 164) points out, the type of relationship that the Commission has noted between the Endorois and their lands is a relationship that 'includes the duty of stewardship'. The Commission stressed that 'validation of rights is not automatically afforded to ... pre-invasion and pre-colonial claims',[24] as indigenous peoples must also 'have an unambiguous relationship to a distinct territory and that all attempts to define [them] recognise the linkages between people, their land, and culture'.[25] The Commission did not simply recognize group rights to lands on the ground of historical occupancy. It also provided 'extensive treatment ... of the cultural, spiritual and, in effect "all-encompassing relationships" between peoples and territories' (Bavikatte 2014: 167). Had there been evidence of ecologically destructive activities by the communities, the courts might have more likely recognized compensations for the eviction, rather than rights over the lands and natural resources (Bavikatte 2014: 168).

Another recent case, not mentioned by Bavikatte, where the protection of indigenous peoples rights was brought forward in association with the protection of the environment is the Niyamgiri case, decided by the Indian Supreme Court in 2013.[26] In 2004, the Indian Ministry of Environment and Forest (MoEF) approved a project of the UK-based mining company M/s Sterlite, parent company of Vedanta

---

[23] *Endorois Welfare Council*, para 235.

[24] *Endorois Welfare Council*, para 154.

[25] *Endorois Welfare Council*, para 154.

[26] *Orissa Mining Corporation Ltd. v. Ministry of Environment & Forests & Others* (2013) Writ Petition (Civil) No. 180 of 2011 (hereinafter referred to as *Orissa Mining Corporation*). I owe thanks to one of the reviewers of this book for the suggestion to examine this interesting case.

Resources, for the construction of an alumina refinery and a coal thermal plant on the eastern coast of India, based on the assurance that the project would not have a detrimental effect on the local forest.[27]

In the meantime, Vedanta Resources applied for authorization to start the mining of bauxite (an aluminium ore) in an area close to Sterlite's project. Its site of extraction was meant to be the Niyamgiri Hills, where a forest rich in biodiversity and hosting many species labelled as endangered in the IUCN Red List is located. The forest also happens to be the main source of livelihood for the Dongaria Kondh and Kutia Kondh tribes,[28] which are so-called 'Scheduled Tribes', entitled to special protection under Indian law. The tribes consider the forest sacred, regard it as inhabited by the deity Niyam Raja, and perceive its conservation as essential for their survival as communities. In fact, the remarkable preservation of the forest is due to the existence of a community ban on cutting its trees (Chandra 2016a). Unsurprisingly, the mining project provoked passionate local protests.

Given that the mining project involved the diversion of forest to allow the creation of the mine, the Forest Advisory Committee had to be consulted. The Supreme Court, hearing the report of the Committee, noted in 2007 that the project would actually negatively affect the local forest and communities and stated that it 'might consider granting clearance to the project' only if Vedanta agreed to comply with a rehabilitation package, which included: sharing a percentage of annual profits for Scheduled Area Development, fund the local Wildlife Management Plan, and provide permanent jobs.[29] Vedanta accepted the rehabilitation package, hence the Supreme Court cleared, in 2008, the forest diversion proposal to undertake

---

[27] *Orissa Mining Corporation*, para 3.

[28] *Orissa Mining Corporation*, para 9 and 14.

[29] *Orissa Mining Corporation*, para 7.

mining, and the MoEF followed suit with its approval.[30] However, Vedanta needed final approval from the Forest Advisory Committee. The Committee appointed an expert committee, the Saxena Committee, to further explore the impact of the project.[31] The report stated that the Dongaria Kondh and Kutia Kondh tribes had not been consulted, that the bauxite extraction would harm their spiritual beliefs, and that it contravened the Scheduled Tribes and Other Forest Dwellers (Recognition of Forest Rights) Act, 2006, as well as the Forest Conservation Act, 1980 and the Environmental Protection Act, 1986.[32]

The MoEF decided to follow the report and, in 2010, withdrew the authorization for the mining process. Shortly after, another petition was brought before the Supreme Court against the MoEF's decision to withdraw the authorization. With the 2013 judgment, the Supreme Court confirmed the MoEF's decision, noting that 'forests have the best chance to survive if communities participate in their conservation and regeneration measures'[33] and recognizing that, under the Scheduled Tribes and Other Forest Dwellers Act, the *gram sabhas* (village assemblies) retained the right to determine whether or not to proceed with the mining: all the 12 interested gram sabhas voted against it (Marshall and Balaton-Chrimes 2016: 21).

[30]   *Orissa Mining Corporation*, para 11.

[31]   *Orissa Mining Corporation*, para 13.

[32]   *Orissa Mining Corporation*, paras 14–15. The Scheduled Tribes and Other Forest Dwellers (Recognition of Forest Rights) Act, 2006 is the result of an uneasy compromise reached between 'hard-line urban wildlife neo-conservationists', distrustful of local communities' management of natural resources and lands, and local communities claiming for the recognition of the rights to live, use, and manage their traditional forests; see Chandra (2016a).

[33]   *Orissa Mining Corporation*, para 42.

This decision is particularly interesting because it sheds light on the significance of Scheduled Tribes and Other Forest Dwellers Act, for the combined protection of indigenous peoples and environmental interests. The Niyamgiri case was the first in which the Act was implemented to recognize the rights of communities involved to not only the right of prior informed consent but an actual veto power over a mining project (Chandra 2016a). The Act recognizes the rights of scheduled tribes and other traditional forest dwellers[34]—also in the absence of a legal title—to live in the forest, to ownership of the land, to use forest resources, of access and use biodiversity, to intellectual property and traditional knowledge related to biodiversity and cultural diversity, to be preserved from destructive practices affecting their cultural and natural heritage, and 'to regulate access to community forest resources and stop any activity which adversely affects the wild animals, forest and the biodiversity'.[35]

Furthermore, the Act recognizes the right of communities to 'protect, regenerate, or conserve or manage any community forest resource, which they have been traditionally protecting and conserving for sustainable use',[36] including the protection of wildlife, forests, and biodiversity. The latter set of rights complement other forest rights with a set of responsibilities towards the environment. The communities' rights are not only recognized due to traditional occupancy, but they are also called, de facto, to act as stewards of their forests trough the empowerment of local authorities, the gram sabha. Though the Act still includes many unclear passages (Chandra 2016a), together

---

[34] According to the Act, 'other traditional forest dweller' means 'any member or community who has for at least three generations prior to the 13th day of December, 2005 primarily resided in and who depends on the forest or forests land for *bona fide* livelihood needs' (Chapter 1.2).

[35] Scheduled Tribes and Other Forest Dwellers Act, chapters 2.3 and 3.5.

[36] Scheduled Tribes and Other Forest Dwellers Act, chapter 2.3.

with the Supreme Court decision, it represents a step towards the combination of rights of indigenous peoples and local communities with environmental responsibilities, in line with the imaginary wire of biocultural rights designed by Bavikatte.

Apparently very different but, according to this author's view, of similar importance for the debate on biocultural rights, is the case of the recognition of rights to the Whanganui River in New Zealand. Resulting from a countless number of court cases, parliamentary petitions, interventions of the Waitangi Tribunal[37] and reports (Iorns Magallanes 2015), the case was settled first by the Whanganui River Agreement of 2012, and then with the adoption of the Te Awa Tupua (Whanganui River Claims Settlement) Act, 2017.

The Te Awa Tupua Act begins with a formal apology of the Crown for failing to respect the Waitangi Treaty signed with the Maori tribes in 1840, which recognized the Maori as legitimate possessors and guardians of their lands and natural resources, including the Whanganui river. Regardless of the treaty, in fact, the river beds, waters, and shores have been extensively used, modified, and exploited without the consent, but with the sharp opposition, of the indigenous peoples living along the river, the Whanganui *iwi* (tribe). The Te Awa

---

[37] The Waitangi Tribunal is a commission that makes recommendations on the application of the Treaty of Waitangi with the aim of guiding legislative and judiciary decisions. The Treaty of Waitangi is the treaty that was signed between the British Crown and the Maori in 1840. The Treaty established the terms of British colonial settlement and the recognition of Maori lands and resources. However, it has been object of strong controversies since its signature because of the breaches that the New Zealand government perpetuated. For example, in the *Wi Parata* judgment of 1877 the Supreme Court declared the Treaty null (Richardson 2008: 25) and by 1990 the Maori had lost most of their lands and resources (Walker 2012: 24). The Tribunal was established precisely to promote the respect of the Treaty.

Tupua Act recognizes that the alteration of the river has caused significant prejudice to the special relationship of the Whanganui iwi with the river and undermined their ability to fulfil their responsibilities towards the river as well as in exercising their customary rights.

The iwi, in fact, regard the river not just as a natural resource, but as one of their ancestors, a living being, to be protected, respected, and guarded for the physical, cultural, and spiritual survival of their communities (Hsiao 2012: 371). The iwi have a set of customary laws concerning the dos and don'ts on the river, with rules that forbid, for example, the mixture of its waters with unclean waters (where 'unclean' means human waste water, even after treatment, which would be considered non-environmentally harming according to Western standards). It is therefore not surprising that the Whanganui iwi have been doing all in their power to end the construction of dams, the introduction of invasive species for fishing, and the destruction of local eel weirs to allow navigation by steamboats (Hsiao 2012).

In the Te Awa Tupua Act, Te Awa Tupua—which comprises the Whanganui river, all its tributaries, and their beds—is recognized as an indivisible and living whole with legal personality. Te Awa Tupua now holds all the powers, rights, duties, and liabilities of a legal person and exercises them through the Te Pou Tupua office. The Te Pou Tupua is composed of a person nominated by the Whanganui iwi and one to act on behalf of the Crown and its role is to be the human face of the river, to foster its health and interests and to engage with the Whanganui iwi and *hapu* (sub-tribes) as a way to recognize their invaluable contribution to Te Awa Tupua.

Interestingly, the Te Awa Tupua Act recognizes as members of the Whanganui iwi those descendants of the local tribes (Ruatipua, Paerangi, or Haunui-ā-Pāpārangi) who have exercised customary rights and responsibilities with respect to the Whanganui river. The Act acknowledges that the river is a source of physical and spiritual significance for the iwi, and that the concept of Te Awa Tupua strengthens their responsibilities in 'relation to the care, protection, management, and use' (Part 3, clause 69) of the river in accordance with their customary laws, values, and practices. The Act represents an attempt to encapsulate in state law the world views and culture of the Maori people through the recognition of a river as a subject not only worthy of protection but also holding legal standing.

Moreover, the Te Awa Tupua Act provides formal recognition of the role that the Whanganui iwi have performed, against all odds, to protect the river and its ecosystem, and a call to continue that role through their integration in the Te Pou Tupua office, which is entrusted with fulfilling and promoting the interest of the Te Awa Tupua. Given its recent adoption, it is still too early to judge whether it will truly foster a combination of indigenous peoples and environmental interests without neglecting one of the two—especially as the role and decision-making power of the iwi is shared with the government. However, the Act does move in the direction invoked by biocultural rights.

Some Caveats

The documents, cases, and laws cited here are not, in any way, expected to be comprehensive. They are cited to show that the concept of biocultural rights is not simply the product of a wish or aspiration of Bavikatte, but that it aligns with several pieces of the discussion, rhetoric, and jurisprudence on issues related to conservation of the environment and the contribution of indigenous peoples and local communities. These treaties, conventions, declarations, court cases, and laws are in fact very significant for the development of the concept of biocultural rights. They are nature-centred and propose indigenous practices as not only relevant for indigenous peoples' and local communities' identities and development, but also as instrumental for conservation of the environment. They demand states to accord certain rights to them, in particular, in the management of natural resources and for preservation of their traditional knowledge.

These declarations, treaties, and cases do not use the term biocultural rights, nor do they specifically aim at raising a set of rights and duties fully matching the concept of biocultural rights. Nevertheless, the content and form of the rights, the interests and values these documents uphold correspond with the spirit of biocultural rights—they approach the interests of indigenous peoples and local communities as inextricably linked with their lands and natural resources, and picture them as actors dependent on, as well as beneficial for, the environment. They are treated as possessors of ethical approaches, knowledge, and wills, which are different from, and more environmentally sound, than those of mainstream society.[38]

Being and Remaining Stewards of the Environment

The Ancestors: Traditional Resource Rights

The reader might have had the feeling that she has already read something similar in the literature on the rights of indigenous peoples and local communities. The special focus of biocultural rights on the

---

[38] It is important to notice that the UNDRIP is not cited here because its angle and focus are different. Besides acknowledging that indigenous peoples possess knowledge, culture, and practices that contribute to the sustainable use and management of the environment (Preamble), in Article 25, the UNDRIP explicitly recognizes the importance of rights associated with lands, waters and territories: 'Indigenous peoples have the right to maintain and strengthen their distinctive spiritual relationship with their traditionally owned or otherwise occupied and used lands, territories, waters and coastal seas and other resources and to uphold their responsibilities to future generations in this regard.' However, this recognition is clearly founded on the paramount importance of the survival, development, and flourishing of indigenous peoples, and not on their role in conservation of the environment. It would hence be erroneous to suggest that UNDRIP promotes a set of rights and duties along with the spirit of biocultural rights, which build also on an

environment reminds us of their very important ancestors: traditional resource rights (TRRs).[39] Biocultural rights are, however, different in their foundations and consequently in their implications, for the good and for the bad. According to Bavikatte (2014: 235), 'The concept of biocultural rights further nuances Posey's ideas on TRR by introducing stewardship as the fundamental ethos that binds together the different rights that communities need to protect their way of life.' A few words on TRRs are hence necessary to further illustrate the distinctiveness of biocultural rights.

TRRs are baskets, or 'bundles' (Posey 1996), of rights as envisaged by Posey, later joined by Graham Dutfield, in the 1990s (Posey 1990, 1996, 1998, 1999a; Posey and Dutfield 1996). The term 'traditional' is used to refer to the practices, beliefs, customs, knowledge, and cultural heritage of communities living in close relationship with the earth, while the term 'resources' stands for knowledge, technology, aesthetic and spiritual qualities, and tangible and intangible resources necessary for the communities to survive and flourish (Posey and Dutfield 1996: 3). TRRs build on the idea that indigenous peoples and local communities[40] live in a sacred balance (Posey 2002: 3) with the

---

environmental foundation. The rights recognized by UNDRIP are purely, and strongly, human (group) rights.

[39] Posey's ideas and many writings on TRRs recently were object of an extensive study and analysis in the article by Jonas and Shrumm (2012), which was very useful for developing this analysis.

[40] In his publications, Posey uses the following terms interchangeably: 'indigenous peoples', 'local communities', and 'traditional societies'; see Posey (1996, 1999b), 'native peoples', 'indigenous societies', and 'indigenous groups'; see Posey (1990), 'indigenous and traditional peoples'; see Posey and Dutfield (1996), 'local communities', 'indigenous and traditional peoples'; see Posey (1998). The lack of consistency in the terms used may be explained by the fact that Posey decided to focus on the special connection with the environment as the main feature to identify the subjects

environment and that, in order to survive and flourish, such peoples and communities need recognition as holders of not only basic human rights, but also as holders of rights over lands and resources, rights to self-determination, and rights over their cultural and spiritual knowledge and values (Posey 1999b). According to Posey (1996: 15), the TRRs bundle includes all the resources 'that sustain communal identity, express history, are manifest in nature and life, sustain the pride of unique heritage, maintain a healthy environment, and from which emerge sacred and spiritual values'.

Posey (1990) was inspired to develop the concept of TRRs because of the increasing need of indigenous peoples and local communities to find alternative economic resources to survive, develop, and demand respect for their rights vis-à-vis national governments. Most importantly, Posey (1990: 14) noted that indigenous peoples and local communities had no other option than to 'revert to ecological destruction, associated with atrophy of their own knowledge systems, in order to acquire the economic power they need to survive'. The only means of income of indigenous peoples and local communities, such as logging activities, selling off of lands, and commercial hunting, 'require the destruction of tropical forests in order to be obtained' (Posey 1990: 14).

As a way to provide an alternative, Posey called for the recognition of rights over traditional knowledge. Through his years of ethnobio-logical and anthropological research he was able to acknowledge the richness of indigenous knowledge about ecosystems and biodiversity, and witnessed its continuing loss. He denounced how inestimable such loss is both for the communities and the rest of the world:

---

holders of TRRs: 'The debate over who is indigenous should not side-track the important task of valuing local communities ... to rekindle and enhance the spiritual and cultural values that cultures have used effectively to conserve biodiversity'; see Posey (1999a: 4). For consistency, this book will continue to use the term 'indigenous peoples and local communities'.

'[W]ith the disappearance of each indigenous group the world loses an accumulated wealth of millennia of human experience and adaptation' Posey (1990: 14). Posey proposed bioprospecting—the use of traditional knowledge to discover, develop, and improve pharmaceutical, cosmetic, alimentary, and other products—to support indigenous peoples' survival and development in non-destructive ways and promote the conservation of their knowledge. He criticized the fact that none of the revenues of markets based on traditional knowledge flowed back to peoples and communities (Posey 1990). He described this process, later defined as 'biopiracy', as 'the latest—and ultimate—neo-colonial form of exploitation of native peoples' (Posey 1999: 15). He wondered how indigenous peoples, especially new generations, could defend traditional knowledge if it 'offers little economic benefit to indigenous groups caught in the economic maze of consumerism and basic survival?' (Posey 1990: 14) Therefore, Posey called for the recognition of their rights to sharing the benefits arising from the use of their traditional knowledge.

Posey was one of the first scholars to call for the recognition of the right to 'benefit sharing', when the CBD had not yet been written. Posey then expanded the idea of TRRs beyond the protection of traditional knowledge and benefit sharing, and integrated them with otherwise diverse provisions in order to create bundles of rights to address more all-encompassing economic, human rights, and environmental concerns of indigenous peoples and local communities (Posey 1995: 5–6). In particular, Posey focused on the importance of promoting the rights to self-determination and cultural diversity (Posey and Dutfield 1996: 95). His bundle of TRRs included respect for cultural differences and traditional institutions, and prior informed consent and veto power over projects that may affect the lives and livelihoods of indigenous peoples and local communities (Posey 1995: 4).

Posey's formulation of the idea of TRRs was a milestone in the development of the discourse about the rights of indigenous peoples and local communities in relation to the environment. The environment was introduced as an essential element for their survival and flourishing because of their special relationship with it. Posey's work was emphatically directed towards upholding the interests of peoples and communities and, in order to achieve the realization of this aim, he emphasized the need to grant them rights over the environment.

In the TRR formulation, the environment is conceptualized as being instrumental for the protection of interests of indigenous peoples and local communities. The foundational justification of TRRs is precisely the importance that self-determination, and preservation and development of cultural diversity and identity have for indigenous peoples and local communities. The protection of the environment figures as an element which has an instrumental value, which is needed for the realization of certain (very important) interests of indigenous peoples and local communities (Posey and Dutfield 1996: 95). In the biocultural rights construction, instead, conservation of the environment seems to figure as one of their very foundations, to be protected through the affirmation of 'the stewardship of communities [and peoples] over their lands and waters' (Bavikatte and Bennett 2015: 28). The following sections elaborate on the meaning of treating conservation of the environment as a foundation in itself.

A Double Foundation

It is important at this stage to further note the implicit duality at the heart of the concept of biocultural rights, and to try to understand what it means that it has two justificatory premises, two raisons d'être, two foundations considered so important to hold somebody else under duties.[41]

---

[41] See the section titled 'Human Rights from Scratch' in Chapter 2 of this book.

As for the first foundation—the promotion and conservation of the cultural identity and self-determination of indigenous peoples and local communities—it is relatively straightforward to regard it as a very important interest of indigenous peoples and local communities. Cultural identity and self-determination have been and still are the cornerstone of indigenous peoples' struggles for their rights, as they have been regarded as the very building material to construct the realization and protection of all other interests. As in any classical account of group rights, the intrinsic value of the individual group members is coupled with the intrinsic value recognized to the group itself. It is argued that a certain interest of the group and its members is very significant for their survival, well-being, and development and is, hence, important enough to hold somebody else under duties.

The second foundation—protection of the environment—is more complex because it raises doubts about whose interest protection of the environment is: is it only an interest of indigenous peoples and local communities or is it a distinguishable concern?

If protection of the environment were incorporated into biocultural rights as merely an interest of indigenous peoples and local communities it would be significant as long as it was beneficial for the full realization of the first foundation, which is to protect certain interests of indigenous peoples and local communities. The conservation of environment would be relevant as long as it was relevant for indigenous peoples' and local communities' self-determination and for the conservation and development of their cultural identity. There is no doubt that indigenous peoples and local communities not only benefit from the environment, but also actually need it for their very survival as distinct peoples and communities. In fact, as we saw above, many of the indigenous rights that have been fought for are concerning lands and natural resources. But if protection of the environment is incorporated in the biocultural rights construction, merely as an interest of indigenous peoples and local communities, the second foundation collapses on the first: it would become an appendix of it.

A second foundation collapsing on the first seems too limited an account of Bavikatte's concept of biocultural rights and their significance. If this were the case, in fact, it would be hard to argue that conservation of the environment forms a distinct second foundation. But Bavikatte states this clearly: 'biocultural rights base their claims on two foundations' (Bavikatte and Robinson 2011: 50). He claims that 'biocultural rights differ significantly from other group rights [such as indigenous rights] in that the nature of the rights they seek to assert is not necessarily based on ethnicity, religion or minority status but instead on a history of stewardship' (Bavikatte and Bennett 2015: 27) and 'they presuppose an explicit link to the conservation and the sustainable use of biological diversity' (Bavikatte and Bennett 2015: 10).

Bavikatte (2014: 234) presents a visual representation of biocultural rights in the form of 'a wheel with the circumference being the objective of conservation and sustainable use, the central hub being the ethic of stewardship and the spokes being the different biocultural rights that communities require to protect their ways of life [pulling together] seemingly disparate rights in order to achieve the objective of conservation.' The rights in the basket are the spokes that, by protecting certain interests of indigenous peoples and local communities, protect the central hub. The central hub is the ethic of stewardship that, overall, leads (or, better, allows) indigenous peoples and local communities to conserve the environment. In order to give a satisfactory interpretation of Bavikatte's work it therefore seems necessary to treat conservation of the environment as a real foundation, not as a mere appendix of the first foundation relevant only as an interest of indigenous peoples and local communities.

Besides, if the concept of biocultural rights were simply described as a basket of specific rights of indigenous peoples and local communities over environmental assets it might be seen as a simple reproduction of the idea of TRRs. Given the fact that TRRs are more widely known and carry the legacy of Posey, TRRs would probably prove a more influential tool for deployment in the rhetoric of human rights.

If conservation of the environment is not to be regarded as solely an interest of indigenous peoples and local communities, how should it then be conceived? The more plausible answers, it seems, are the following two.

The general conservation of biodiversity, preservation of the dynamic equilibrium of ecosystems, safeguarding the health of air, water, and soil are the very goals of the environment-related documents from which biocultural rights seem to emerge. These documents, more or less explicitly, aim at protecting the interest of humankind (and consequently of states) towards conservation of the environment.[42] According to this interpretation, humankind is the holder of protected interest, hence the holder of intrinsic value whose benefit is sought. The structure of biocultural rights that derives from this understanding is anthropocentric because the environment appears as an asset to be protected for the sake of human beings.

Alternatively, we could adopt a non-anthropocentric approach. Some documents, such as the CBD, used to argue for the emergence of biocultural rights do refer to the intrinsic value of nature in their preambles. It could hence be suggested that biocultural rights are justified by conservation of the environment because the latter has an intrinsic value to be protected.[43]

---

[42] The CBD and the Nagoya Protocol, the Rio Declaration and Agenda 21, and the other international treaties and declarations cited above are grounded on the idea that the environment is to be protected for the sake of humankind, in order to respond to its current needs and the needs of future generations; see Sands et al. (2012: 776).

[43] This second interpretation can be understood in two ways. First, conservation of the environment is treated as a value to be protected through biocultural rights: duties are due in order to protect a value, which is not

The first option could prove to be more rhetorically powerful, as the language of international and national law mostly remains anthropocentric. The second, embracing non-anthropocentric ethical approaches, could instead appear closer to the world views and legal systems of indigenous peoples and local communities. For the purpose of this book, the description of the second foundation as either anthropocentric or not may remain unspecified. Importantly, whether conservation of the environment is regarded as a value per se or an interest of humankind, it seems possible to picture biocultural rights as constructed upon two real foundations. Accordingly, indigenous peoples and local communities are granted a set of rights, not only, as is in the case of TRRs, for their own survival, development, and flourishing, but also for the survival, development, and flourishing of a far broader human constituency, or for an even broader non-human constituency: humankind or the environment itself.

This duality lends a certain complexity—and foreignness within the human rights rhetoric—to the question of rights and duties, which arise and change according to the way in which the holders of the interest are conceptualized. The duality of their foundation means that biocultural rights are limited to certain categories of rights—and that such rights have a distinctive character driven by

---

somebody's (or something's) interests. According to a second understanding, which requires a further rhetorical shift, the environment is accorded a certain level of subjectivity and is regarded as a subject that can hold rights. The environment becomes one of the right holders of biocultural rights and the duties of sustainability are due to the environment itself. This interpretation stands with that branch of theory and law—still in the minority—that has proposed the enlargement of the human rights discourse to non-human entities (such as the Ecuadorian and Bolivian constitutions or the Te Awa Tupua Act). However, the recognition of environment as a subject seems merely, in this construction, a rhetorical shift.

the imposition of the stewardship duty emerging from the second foundation (conservation of the environment). In fact, as explained below, the rights that respond to the needs and interests of peoples and communities, but have no connection to the maintenance of this broader role as conservationists, cannot be fully justified as bio-cultural rights because they would not build on both foundations. Moreover, the consequences, in terms of the duties arising for the protection of this double foundation, are quite unfamiliar. So unfamiliar—and not explicitly envisaged by Bavikatte—that they might leave us with a feeling of uneasiness in human rights terms. Before moving to the challenging issue concerning duties, it is necessary to explore one side of the coin, the one concerning rights, as it allows us to proceed with more clarity.

Of Rights and Duties

Which Rights for Stewardship?

The biocultural rights discourse is grounded on the assumption that there are indigenous peoples and local communities that have maintained stewardship relationships with the environment. It is now important to understand which conditions exist for a people or com-munity to be free to maintain its traditional way of life and its role as steward of the environment, and, above all, how these conditions for stewardship can be preserved. This is an important question, to which biocultural rights are—in a sense—a response. The basket of biocultural rights would in fact be filled with the 'rights required by communities to care for their lands and resources' (Bavikatte 2014: 235) and to protect their ways of life.

Bavikatte and Robinson (2011: 50) argue that such ways of life are 'linked to secure land tenure, use rights and rights to culture, knowledge and practices'. Since each community and people has different needs in terms of rights to maintain its way of life, the biocultural rights basket cannot be conceptualized as a static set of pre-selected rights: it will necessarily vary from one context to another in response to local circumstances and nuances, which can be expected to exist in relation to communities' and peoples' traditions, to their relationship with local ecosystems, and to their level of interaction or conflict with external actors.

However, environmental stewardship necessarily postulates the protection of certain basic interests of indigenous peoples and local communities, that is, non-discrimination, protection of cultural integrity, self-government, access and use of lands, waters, and natural resources, and social and health welfare. Therefore, although heterogeneous and dynamic, the basket of biocultural rights can be said to be filled with three *categories* of rights, which encompass all the different rights needed to preserve a stewardship relationship with the environment.

1. Rights to Land and Natural Resources: These include the right to access and use of traditional lands and waters; special access to sacred natural sites; access and use over biotic (plants, animals, bacteria, and fungi) and abiotic (water, soil, air, rocks) resources present in the land;[44] protection from external threats to the environment such as pollution, invasive species, and climate change. The conservation and protection of cultural identities, lifestyles, and livelihoods is recognized to be 'contingent on protection and control of traditional land bases and associated natural resources' (Schmidt and Peterson 2009: 1459; Tsosie 1996: 228–32) as the relationship with native lands is a central element to the collective identities and well-being of peoples and communities (Johnston 1995: 193).

---

[44] Rights over underground resources of a land are often kept as the property of the state. In terms of biocultural rights, a community/people's rights over them may need to be secured in order to avoid that their exploitation, by states or private companies, endangering their lifestyles, practices, and traditional knowledge.

Native lands provide not only physical but also spiritual resources, which are necessary for the survival of these communities and peoples as well as for the conservation of their distinctive and sound existence (Johnston 1995: 194). The inextricable link that characterises the relationship between many indigenous peoples and local communities with their lands, waters, and natural resources builds on the recognition of titles over these elements—may they be common property titles or other forms of protection of use, management, and transmission to future generations. If deprived of their lands and natural resources, they become vulnerable and dependent on mainstream society, with the only options of disappearing or vanishing into suburbs, cities, or townships.

2. Rights to Self-determination: The *internal*[45] right to self-determination entails the possibility of each people and community to regulate its internal matters through the use of its legal institutions and rules, which reflect its cultural patterns, such as that the members may generally feel associated with the decisions taken (Anaya 1996: 112). Traditional local institutions regulating the use of lands and natural resources are the primary instrument giving voice and application to the needs, concerns, and interests of the peoples and communities (Maffi 2014: 9). Local institutions are therefore fundamental to the maintenance of traditional knowledge, values, and customary laws and to the intergenerational transmission of language and culture, thus centrally contributing to the enhancement and conservation of the cultural and spiritual practices and beliefs relevant for the protection of the local environment (Maffi 2014: 9).

The intensive interweaving of land and identity has particularly telling implications for the relationship between governmental

---

[45] See the subsection titled 'Indigenous Peoples' Rights' in Chapter 2 of this book, on the distinction between internal and external self-determination and on the relevance of the first for indigenous peoples.

policy and laws and local practices. Precisely because the imposition of governmental policies, laws, and projects can undermine the preservation of traditional institutions, certain degrees of normative autonomy and self-determination are essential to preserve traditional institutions, rules, and commons-like property systems (Tsosie 1996: 293). This is 'to ensure that not only their lands and resources but also their ways of life and livelihoods, institutions and identities, values and knowledge systems, cultural traditions and languages are protected' (Maffi 2014: 9).

To exercise their authority, local institutions need to be recognized as legitimate by members of their community and combined with a certain degree of social cohesion (Tsosie 1996: 289, 294). A lack of social cohesion may make traditional mechanisms such as ostracism, shame, or fear of bad luck ineffective for guiding the behaviour of community members (Tsosie 1996: 289). Accordingly, many scholars and international conservation organizations have recognized that certain degrees of self-determination and control over natural resources are necessary primarily to allow the survival and flourishing of indigenous peoples and local communities, of their identities, lifestyles, and spiritual and cultural traditions, and, consequently, to allow the conservation of their role as stewards of the environment (Anaya 1996: 110; Schmidt and Peterson 2009: 1459).

3. Rights to Cultural Identity: This category refers to those rights necessary to safeguard the integrity of the values and world views, and practices and knowledge of indigenous peoples and local communities. It includes the right to speak traditional languages, to profess religious and spiritual practices, to education of children, and to apply, preserve, and teach traditional knowledge in other words, the broader right to maintain cultural, social, and religious specificities without experiencing discrimination by the state and by the rest of society. It also includes rights in respect of ABS provisions concerning the access and use of traditional knowledge associated

with genetic resources, that is, the right to prior informed consent, to mutually agreed terms, to respecting customary laws and community protocols, and to the fair and equal sharing of the benefits.[46]

Given the intimacy between traditional world views, practices, and cultural identities with indigenous peoples' and local communities' environmental stewardship, these rights are also fundamental to the nature of biocultural rights. A strong cultural identity confers a sense of pride (Maffi 2014: 10) through the identification with a certain heritage. When it is strong and flourishing, cultural identity can foster the conservation of cultural practices, knowledge, and languages that regulate and maintain the sustainable use of lands and natural resources (Maffi 2014: 10). Local traditional languages are one of the major elements of cultural identity and one of the means to communicate and pass on, generation after generation, knowledge of local biodiversity, traditional resource use, and management practices (Maffi 2014: 8).

Besides these substantive rights, procedural rights (such as the right to access to justice, the right to free prior informed consent, and the right to the application of a precautionary approach) would also

---

[46] These rights, which can be subsumed under the label 'ABS rights'—for an analysis of the different uses of the concept of ABS (right, obligation, mechanism, safeguard, and so on), see Morgera (2016)—are an important part of the biocultural rights basket because they determine control and self-government of indigenous peoples and local communities over a fundamental asset of their culture, which is intrinsically linked to the natural resources of their lands. However, the sole recognition of ABS rights would not be enough to guarantee the securing of the stewardship role of peoples and communities over their lands and waters. Other rights, such as the right to land, the right to maintain traditional institutions and decision-making procedures, the right to language and religion, mentioned above, are also 'required to secure the stewardship role of communities over their lands and waters' (Bavikatte 2014: 16).

be essential elements in the basket of biocultural rights because they are the tools that peoples and communities would need in order to prevent or halt violations of biocultural rights. They would be essential for making biocultural rights enforceable and prevent them from merely existing on paper.

Logically, in light of the twofold foundation of biocultural rights, it must not be forgotten that the interests of indigenous peoples and local communities go hand in hand with conservation of the environment. Hence, all the rights just listed can *only* be considered to be part of the basket of biocultural rights if they are relevant to guarantee the stewardship role of indigenous peoples and local communities towards the environment. Clearly, it is impossible to select them a priori, with no reference to a specific people/community, because the basket of biocultural rights, as noted above, changes from one case to another according to local circumstances and nuances. Accordingly, certain rights may not always be justifiable as biocultural rights in a given specific context because they may not always have relevance for conservation of the environment.

Such indeterminacy, however, is neither problematic for the theory of rights—which welcomes the possibility of foundations being protected with different means within a certain range of duties—nor it is dangerous for the concept of biocultural rights. It is in fact possible to identify a core of rights, such as the right to land and natural resources which is necessary for all communities and peoples performing a stewardship function, leaving others, such as the right to language, as possible expansions to be added in specific circumstances. What does remain problematic—and will be further explored in Chapter 5— is that the search for such rights is not solely aimed at fulfilling the interests of indigenous peoples and local communities, but also conservation of the environment.

It could be argued that biocultural rights are nothing more than this—a set—not even very determined—of distinct rights of different subjects, and the corresponding set of duties. This critique fails to see how biocultural rights derive from two common and previously separate foundations and does not recognize the changes resulting from this. It is true that biocultural rights are an assemblage of rights and duties distinguishable from one another, and this is also how they have been described. However, a right does not solely consist of a single legal position, it also consists of its functional unit, which is given by its justificatory premises, its foundations. If old rights are assembled in a new structure with different foundations, their boundaries will change. The reason why the theoretical construct of biocultural rights is appropriate is not because it raises new undebated interests, but because it justifies the protection of these interests on different premises and with different implications.

Duty Holders?

Any analysis of rights requires an equally attentive analysis of the corresponding duties to avoid that rights remain mere pretences (O'Neill 2004: 97). Accordingly, if we want to take biocultural rights seriously[47] and protect their justifying foundations, we need to examine the duties they would give rise to and identify the holders of such duties. In the case of the first foundation (justified by the interest of indigenous peoples and local communities in the promotion of their self-determination and in the conservation of their cultural identity) this matter is relatively clear. The second foundation instead (conservation of the environment, whether as an interest and humankind or as an intrinsic value) requires more complex considerations.

The promotion and conservation of the cultural identity and self-determination of indigenous peoples and local communities is clearly a direct interest they hold. Indigenous peoples and local communities, as holders of the protected interests, are openly the subjects to whom

[47] A rephrasing of the title of the seminal book by Ronald Dworkin, *Taking Rights Seriously.*

the duties would be due. The holders of corresponding duties (both to act and to refrain from acting) would most likely be states, private enterprises, and the international community, since these are most likely to be able to affect the conservation of the cultural identity and the self-determination of indigenous peoples and local communities.

States, for example, would likely have the duty to recognize secure land and resource rights[48] and to respect local institutions, decision-making processes, traditional practices, and world views by refraining from imposing inappropriate levels of state interference, limiting the use of local languages, and forcing conservation, development, educational, or other policies. Private enterprises would likely have the duty to respect the wills of indigenous peoples and local communities on their recognized lands, to act only after free prior informed consent has been sought, and to accept the refusal of projects and other interventions. The international community would also likely have a duty to refrain from imposing conservation or development projects, such as protected areas, unless they are discussed, processed, and accepted by local peoples and communities.

Under these circumstances, indigenous peoples and local communities would be claimants for the fulfilment of the duties to uphold their self-determination and cultural identity rights vis-à-vis national states and their institutions, private enterprises, and the international community. At times, other interested parties could speak on their behalf, as might be the case with non-governmental organizations or community-based organizations, but such parties would always need to be legitimated by the relevant communities or peoples.

The second foundation, protection of the environment, as mentioned above, raises more complex issues. Indigenous peoples and

---

[48] Secure land and resource rights means that the title of the community or people cannot be over-ridden by exploitative concessions or other permits issued by the state (Jonas, Jonas, and Subramanian 2013: 219).

local communities directly benefit from the protection of their environment because they depend on lands and natural resources for their survival and flourishing and for the conservation and development of their cultural identity. If the emergence of biocultural rights is postulated, this implies that such interests are considered important enough to justify placing a duty (to act and to refrain from acting) upon a range of actors to protect the environment. As in the previous case, states and private enterprises are still among the actors most likely to be able to affect the conservation of the environment and therefore to protect this specific interest of indigenous peoples and local communities. Such actors would be obligated not to deplete the lands and natural resources of indigenous peoples and local communities and, under certain conditions, would also have the duty to support remedial actions in degraded areas where biological diversity has been depleted. In this context, indigenous peoples and local communities would also remain claimants for the protection of the environment vis-à-vis states, private enterprises and, in certain cases, the international community.

However, it has been argued that in biocultural rights, conservation of the environment also serves as an autonomous foundation. As noted above, the rights included in the biocultural rights basket are precisely those needed to maintain the stewardship role of indigenous peoples and local communities towards the environment and, consequently, also to protect this general interest or value. In order to understand how this protection is guaranteed, further reflection on the stewardship role of indigenous peoples and local communities seems necessary.

If we assume that indigenous peoples and local communities are and will remain sustainable once their biocultural rights are protected, then the implication is that conservation of the environment is more or less automatically guaranteed once the rights of indigenous peoples and local communities (to lands and natural resources, to self-determination, and to cultural identity) are protected, and the only duties requiring operationalization—in such a situation—would be those of states, private enterprises, and the international community.

However, this is an implication based upon an unstable assumption. Simply providing rights to land and resources, rights to self-determination, and rights to preserve distinct cultural identities does not imply—much less guarantee—that the interested community/people will maintain its sustainable lifestyle forever. Indigenous peoples' and local communities' practices, rules, and beliefs may not always remain 'in line with conservation goals' (Berkes 2004: 625). It is essential that the biocultural rights discourse should keep a distance from the 'noble savage' rhetoric and its ideological trap, because otherwise, conservation of the environment, one of the two foundations of biocultural rights, would not be really taken into consideration. Moreover, any such mythology would leave biocultural rights relatively weak in the face of data showing the potential threat that indigenous peoples and local communities themselves might pose to the environment in certain cases and circumstances.

It is not enough to affirm, as Bavikatte and Bennett (2015: 9) do, that a 'definite empirical proof that recognition and enforcement of biocultural rights promotes better environmental protection remains elusive'. The logic of biocultural rights within Bavikatte's construction suggests that biocultural rights approaches either fall in the ideological trap of the noble savage, or explicitly need to incorporate a duty to remain sustainable (something Bavikatte seems to acknowledge only timidly). If indigenous peoples and local communities were entirely free to change sustainable lifestyles to suit their needs, they might potentially disregard the second foundation of biocultural rights, which is one of the (two) reasons for which they were granted such rights. They might take decisions that lead to unsustainable consequences for their lands and resources, and they may also voluntarily decide to not act as stewards of the environment anymore.

Bavikatte does suggest that biocultural rights incorporate 'an obligation of stewardship' and 'a duty of care and protection' (Bavikatte and Bennett 2015: 11, 21) but he neither elaborates in detail on these statements nor on their consequences. The dual foundations of Bavikatte's formulation—whether located against a stewardship duty on behalf of humankind or on behalf of the value of protection of the environment—present a significant tension and bring major challenges, which are particularly problematic for indigenous peoples, as they are already holders of a different set of rights, *indigenous rights*, which do not present environmental conditions. These challenges, as well as the potential of biocultural rights, are examined in Chapter 5.

5   Biocultural Rights

Handle with Care

A Sui Generis Human Right

Shifting Ethics

Chapter 4 outlined the main features of the concept of biocultural rights[1] and introduced their interesting and challenging specificities. Most intriguingly, it was proposed that the dual foundation of biocultural rights—and biocultural rights

---

[1] It is worth remembering that biocultural rights, even though they are possibly in the process of *emerging*, they are not yet legal rights. Hence, this analysis is not an interpretation of current international, regional, or national law; it is a theoretical discussion on what characteristics they would have and the problems that would arise *if* they came to be recognized by law.

themselves—only appear as fully significant if their second foundation does not collapse on their first: that is, only if conservation of the environment is regarded as a concern distinguishable from the interests of indigenous peoples and local communities. It was underlined how the environment is fundamental for the lives, identities, culture, and self-determination of indigenous peoples and local communities, but it was also stressed that environmental matters seem to figure as an independent value in the concept of biocultural rights—per se or as an interest of humankind.

In the picture that emerges, biocultural rights appear to be sui generis human rights because indigenous peoples and local communities are granted a basket of rights based not only on their interests but also on conservation of the environment. Human rights are often represented as 'trumps' (Dworkin 1984) over considerations of general interest (Waldron 1984: 17): they protect individual or group interests considered so fundamental that they *outplay* the community as a whole and general values. They may only be balanced against other human rights and limited only in exceptional cases (Dworkin 1984: 153).[2] Instead, in the construction of biocultural rights presented here, a set of fundamental interests of the rights holders—self-determination and conservation of cultural identity—is balanced with and restricted, not for the sake of other individual or group human rights, but for a general interest, namely conservation of the environment. Moreover, in biocultural rights the source of limitation is not exceptional (that is, exercised only in extreme circumstances) because it stems from one of their very foundations. The conservation of environment, in fact, is not only a limit on the exercise of biocultural rights: it is—together with the intrinsic value of indigenous peoples and local communities—one of the values/interests to be pursued through their implementation.

---

[2] See also the section titled 'Functioning and Limits of Human Rights' in Chapter 2 of this book.

It does seem possible to try to overcome this tension with human rights theory by suggesting that the concept of biocultural rights should be explicitly understood to operate as a sui generis legal concept and thereby attempt to create a bridge between human rights as commonly understood in Western legal systems, and the ethical approaches and legal systems of indigenous peoples and local communities.[3]

As Bosselmann (2015: 533) notes, the traditional framework of human rights is not at ease with satisfactorily addressing indigenous peoples' 'collective concerns for the ecological integrity' because of its focus on individuals. Western legal systems can be considered to be rights-based (Bobbio 1988: chapter 3), shaped around the aim of enhancing the interests of each individual subject because she or he is perceived as having a self-standing value, which comes before that of the group (Bobbio 1988). In contrast, indigenous peoples' and local communities' legal approaches may be described as duty-based because they are shaped around the aim of safeguarding the existence of the group by ensuring the conformity of individual actions with certain codes or rules (Barsh 1995). Their normative practices rest upon the understanding that no member can survive outside the community (Cullinan 2002: 114; Masolo 2004: 492), and that the community itself cannot survive if detached from the surrounding natural world. Thus, the well-being and general interest of the community depends on the well-being of the environment. Customary laws impose duties and limits to ensure the protection of the community as a whole, future generations, and the individual subject herself or himself.

For as long as it remains true that there is a densely imbricated co-dependency between indigenous peoples and local communities

[3] Given the diversity and richness of the legal systems of indigenous peoples and local communities, much more detailed research would be needed in order to provide for a comprehensive picture of their traditions. Here, an attempt is made to identify some common features, conscious of their very general and superficial nature.

and the local environment, the environmental duties of biocultural rights might not after all be an unacceptable imposition based on environmental expectations incompatible with the commitments of indigenous peoples and local communities. In the traditionally intimate relationship between humans and the environment, the recognition of a stewardship duty might appear to be a step towards the recognition of rights mirroring a fundamental structure of legal approaches and practices of indigenous peoples and local communities at the centre of which there is nature.

However, the fact that indigenous peoples and local communities might change and adapt their customary laws, beliefs, and world views to internal and external changes (such as an encroaching economic system and a globalizing world) includes the possibility that the environment loses its centrality in their legal approaches, values, and norms, or that previously environmentally sound activities become unsustainable because of changes occurring in the surrounding eco-systems (ranging from climate change to migration). Precisely because this might happen, biocultural rights position themselves at an uneasy borderline between rights and conservation of the environment, with potentially unfair implications.

Challenges to Imposing Duties

The dismissal of the 'noble savage' myth leaves us quite unprotected against the idea that biocultural rights would be inherently granting indigenous peoples and local communities not only a basket of rights guaranteeing their freedom to remain sustainable, but also a bundle of duties requiring them to remain sustainable (an 'obligation of steward-ship' as Bavikatte and Bennet (2015: 11) call it). While in the light of relatively static assumptions about the nature of indigenous peoples and local communities such duties may seem to be in line with their legal systems, values, and desires, in a world of changing contexts and complex pressures, such duties could become a burden upon such peoples and communities, in direct conflict with the same rights granted by biocultural rights.

We could seek to counter this objection by emphasizing that the duty to maintain a role as stewards of the environment does not necessarily imply a static perpetuation of traditional ways of life, as the dichotomy between traditional 'natural conservationists' and modern destroyers of the environment suggests.[4] Within the biocultural rights framework, indigenous peoples and local communities would be free to (self-)determine their ways of life, to develop their culture, traditions, and practices in line with their desires, wills, and needs, to adapt to external inputs, and to undertake internal changes. They might, for example, combine their traditions with techniques, knowledge, and practices acquired from other societies. However, it would remain non-negotiable for them to do so while remaining sustainable. This understanding puts biocultural rights in the dangerous position of appearing as yet another instrument to shift the burden of conservation on indigenous peoples and local communities.

A further question arises spontaneously. What happens if a community or people fail to carry out the duty of sustainability? In the most extreme cases of environmental damage it could be argued that they may be subject to the loss of entitlement to biocultural rights because they would in fact lose one of the requirements necessary to be holders of such rights. In less extreme cases, sanctions could be envisaged, but the very idea of a sanction imposed on a community or people appears strongly problematic.

Furthermore, it is hard to define what conception of a protected environment should a people accused of unsustainability be judged on, considering that different concepts of 'environment' and 'sustainable' are held by indigenous peoples, local communities, the conservation science community, and international environmental law itself (Alcorn

---

[4] See also the subsection titled 'From Myth to Reality' in Chapter 3.

1993: 425). The same actions and projects may be considered sustainable or unsustainable depending on the concept they are measured against, and, even more debatable, depending on the body entitled to judge them.

The subject for whose sake the sustainability duty exists—be it humankind or the environment—is not a definite entity, with the capacity to require enforcement of rights and duties. It needs a representative[5] and the most likely representatives are states and some elements of civil society (non-governmental organizations, community-based organizations, foundations, and the like) that might claim to represent such general interest. This approach of representation produces strong tensions and bears the risk of getting carried away by misconceptions. Granting full trust to states, which are the most likely representatives, is in danger of falling for the myth of the 'noble state' (Alcorn 1993: 424). States' practices, although having improved over the last few years, cannot as yet create full trust (Stevens 2014: 4), as they have a colonial and postcolonial history of disregarding indigenous peoples' and local communities' rights and have often shown the 'lack of the necessary capacity, resources, or political will' (Stevens 2014: 4) to properly achieve conservation outcomes.

From what we have seen so far, we can elicit the following points: the rights to lands and natural resources, self-determination, and cultural identity subsumed under the concept of biocultural rights are limited by sustainability considerations and come with duties; it is hard to understand who should be entitled to judge the enforcement of such environmental duties and it is even harder to delineate what sanctions could be envisaged for their violation; we move on uneasy ground when considering the very definition of sustainability to be applied;

---

[5] The difficulty of finding an appropriate claimant is shown by the fact that even the task of determining claimants of constitutionally embedded human environmental rights is very challenging. For an introductory reconstruction of the issue, see May and Daly (2011).

and we are in danger of imposing unfair environmental burdens on indigenous peoples and local communities. Consequently, these points pose an imperative question: is the concept of biocultural rights actually a good idea? In order to answer this question, a distinction is required to be made between the two possible holders of biocultural rights—indigenous peoples and local communities—because they find themselves in very different positions concerning rights and their linkages with conservation of the environment.

A Good Idea(?)

Indigenous Peoples *or* Local Communities: A Necessary Distinction

The traditional intimacy between indigenous peoples and local communities and their living environments and natural resources, acknowledged by indigenous peoples and local communities themselves, is a strong reason why an engagement with biocultural rights as an emergent category of human rights is important to address. When placed within the existing human rights and environmental debate, it is a promising approach to address the current global environmental crisis while not reverting to 'fortress conservation' actions (Brechin et al. 2002). That being said, it is important to acknowledge that placing so much emphasis on the relationship between indigenous peoples and local communities and the environment requires us to bear in mind a warning: 'Above all, it seems to me wrongheaded and dangerous to invoke historical assumptions about environmental practices of native peoples in order to justify treating them fairly.... By invoking this assumption to justify fair treatment of native peoples, we imply that it would be OK to mistreat them if that assumption could be refuted' (Diamond 2005: 10).

To emphasize the role of indigenous peoples and local communities in protection of the environment does indeed present the danger of subordinating their rights to environmental considerations.

Biocultural rights, as conceived by Bavikatte (and drawn from environment-related international documents and agreements) cannot evade this danger, since they are precisely based on indigenous peoples' and local communities' stewardship role towards ecosystems and biodiversity. How then, might this risk be addressed?

Most importantly, this risk implies the need to draw a distinction between indigenous peoples and local communities. The concept of biocultural rights as presented by Bavikatte refers to both indigenous peoples and local communities, and the two groups are co-referents for the same umbrella of rights. Jonas, Makagon, and Shrumm (2013: 26), by contrast, suggest that biocultural rights may eventually be appropriate to describe the claims that local communities are making, while certainly not the claims of indigenous peoples. This suggestion hinges on the special dependency of local community rights on environmental contexts—a factor distinguishing them from indigenous peoples, which instead possess a special recognition in *their own right*.[6] Despite the fact that the Inter-American Court on Human Rights has recently recognized certain indigenous rights to local communities (Antkowiak 2007), the latter cannot so far be regarded as holding the same rights or status of indigenous peoples (Jonas, Makagon, and Shrumm 2013: 26). Local communities, unlike indigenous peoples, currently lack complete recognition in international law and have only recently been gaining acknowledgement.

Since their first appearance in international law, in Article 8j of the CBD,[7] local communities have appeared in many other international documents *because of* their relationship with the environment. They are considered, in other words, precisely because of their role in the conservation of certain environmental assets or ecosystems—not because of their existence as communities. For

---

[6] See the subsection titled 'Rights of Indigenous Peoples' in Chapter 2.

[7] See the subsection titled 'Rights of Local Communities' in Chapter 2.

such communities, therefore, the linking of biocultural rights and stewardship duties might not present the same kind of dangers as it does for indigenous peoples.

By contrast, indigenous peoples are holders of indigenous rights and 'can exercise certain rights under international law regardless of the type of lifestyle they lead' (Jonas, Makagon, and Shrumm 2013: 26). They can claim indigenous rights, widely recognized in international law, purely because of their *indigenous status* and regardless of their stewardship role towards the environment (Jonas, Makagon, and Shrumm 2013). The foundation of indigenous rights 'is an extensive connection to the land of their ancestors and the critical importance that has for their identities and contemporary ways of life' (Jonas, Makagon, and Shrumm 2013: 23). Such rights do *not* arise from environmentally related considerations and do not bind their holders to any conservation-oriented conduct: 'indigenous rights were developed within the framework of general human rights' (Jonas, Makagon, and Shrumm 2013: 23) and, as such, they are to be specially secured. Biocultural rights, by contrast, are sui generis human rights based, also, on a general interest for the value of conservation of the environment. Therefore, for Jonas, Makagon, and Shrumm (2013), unlike for Bavikatte and Robinson (2011), indigenous peoples do not hold biocultural rights.

According to this author's view, whether indigenous peoples are holders of biocultural rights or not is a matter of definition. The concept of biocultural rights, as conceptualized by Bavikatte, is based on the words of the CBD, the Nagoya Protocol, and other international documents referring to indigenous peoples, local communities, farmers, traditional communities, and the like. Under this definition of biocultural rights, those indigenous peoples, as well as those local communities that have preserved sustainable lifestyles, which are relevant for conservation of the environment, would meet the requirements to be regarded as holders of biocultural rights. Indigenous peoples remain, of course, holders of indigenous rights as well. The conflation of two or more subjects as holders of a same set of rights, or the addition of a new set of rights to the legal landscape of a holder, does not restrict the holders' rights.[8]

A more pressing issue concerns whether it would be strategically helpful for indigenous peoples to ask for the recognition of biocultural rights, or whether they might incur more costs than benefits by framing their claims in these terms. In other words, can biocultural rights improve the chances of indigenous peoples seeing their interests protected and counteract a history of marginalization? This issue brings us back to the conclusion of the last section and the question: are biocultural rights a good idea?

First and foremost, the recognition of biocultural rights would not enhance the legal position of indigenous peoples under international law. They are already holders of the rights included in the basket of biocultural rights as holders of indigenous rights, which are recognized in international law and are protected by international courts (such as the Inter-American Court on Human Rights, the African Court on Human and Peoples' Rights, and the European Court of Human Rights). Moreover, indigenous rights do not require their holders to live a sustainable lifestyle, nor do they imply any duty to conserve the environment. Indigenous peoples' rights are limited, like all other human rights, but only by conflicting human rights and by laws and regulations protecting very important aspects of public interest (for example, the right to self-determination of an indigenous people may be limited by state laws concerning toxic wastes and possession of firearms). On the contrary, the right to self-determination that would be conferred as part of the biocultural rights basket is limited also by the duty to be and remain sustainable.

---

[8] Similarly, women, who are holders of women's rights, can also be holders of workers' rights, shared with men—and the two sets of rights do not restrict one another.

This very delicate point requires some rhetorical and political considerations. To talk about indigenous peoples in conjunction with environmental concerns might bear the risk of leading judges, politicians, and activists to expect indigenous peoples to live sustainable lifestyles in order to be accorded not only biocultural rights but also indigenous rights. Hence, the use of biocultural rights arguments to promote indigenous interests could present the danger of conditioning indigenous rights to environmental considerations, rather than to their extensive connection to ancestral lands and indigeneity alone. The rhetoric of indigenous rights may be infiltrated by environmental stewardship duties, riding the wave of the rhetoric picturing indigenous peoples as particularity interested in conservation of the environment.

Such consequence is not, however, implied in the concept of biocultural rights. It is an unintended consequence which should be taken into consideration when dealing with biocultural rights. Some may say that if this danger is acknowledged, then this author should have refrained from writing about biocultural rights, thereby potentially contributing to this unintended consequence. This critique could be well placed if this book were an open defence of biocultural rights. But this book is aimed precisely at revealing the main features, potential advantages, *and dangers* of biocultural rights, as stated right from the beginning. The only critique publicly received so far against biocultural rights was raised by Jonas, Makagon, and Shrumm, which dismissed indigenous peoples as potential holders of biocultural rights. This book, instead, works with the very skeleton of biocultural rights, explaining *why* they might be dangerous for indigenous peoples but also avoiding 'throwing out the baby with the bath water', providing details of the developments biocultural rights entail for the debate about human rights and the environment.

Strategic Thinking and Rhetoric

Despite the dangers described above, it is possible that under certain conditions, demanding the recognition of rights under the label of biocultural rights could be *strategically* useful both for local communities and indigenous peoples.

There still exist states using minority language to refer to indigenous peoples (Xanthaki 2007: 133), or denying their very existence, making the indigenous people struggle to exit disadvantaged conditions harder or impossible. Biocultural rights rhetoric can sound more politically neutral and hence be more widely accepted, because, as Bavikatte and Robinson (2011: 50) indicate, biocultural rights do not carry the 'undertone of self-determination that made states nervous'. This is precisely because biocultural rights 'were predominantly lobbied for ... as "environmental rights" of communities to ensure biodiversity conservation' Bavikatte and Robinson (2011: 50), thus directing governments' attention towards environmental and human rights issues rather than to self-determination claims.

Second, many developing countries are facing a strong call from the international community for the conservation of environment within their territories. Many states struggle to address this call because of limited economic resources and because they are also called upon to promote the costly implementation of rights to health, education, food, and water. A state might therefore be more inclined to respond to a call for biocultural rights rather than to a direct call for indigenous rights: biocultural rights simultaneously address a human rights issue, accompanied by the *compensation* of reducing environmental conservation costs.

Third—and relevant for local communities as well—biocultural rights could be a strategic instrument to help indigenous peoples and local communities protect their ways of life through a much-needed 'landscape approach'[9] as an answer to the current fragmentation

---

[9] The 'landscape approach' proposes finding appropriate rights of certain communities or peoples by looking at the different human and natural elements of the landscape where they live; see Jonas, Jonas, and Makagon (2014). It is

of national and international law. Although there are currently an increasing number of laws, programmes, and declarations concerning indigenous peoples and local communities, and protection of the environment, which are providing for rights regarding access to land, benefit sharing, traditional knowledge, carbon emissions, protected areas, and much more, they are essentially fragmented, addressed by different bodies, and found in diverse sources and categories of law (Jonas, Jonas, and Makagon 2014). At present, indigenous peoples and local communities have to engage with a plethora of legal sources in order to protect interconnected aspects of their lives—all part of the same biocultural landscape (Jonas, Jonas, and Makagon 2014).

This process of fragmentation of the local landscape by national and international law is one of the reasons why Posey developed his TRRs approach (Jonas and Shrumm 2012) and looked for a more comprehensive body of law that specifically addresses the overall issues of indigenous peoples and local communities (Jonas, Jonas, and Makagon 2014: 3–5). Bavikatte's deployment of rights under one umbrella label has the advantage of sustaining the political hope of presenting a single interdependent and comprehensive call: a claim for

---

an evolution of the 'ecosystem approach' proposed by the CBD. The latter was presented as an alternative to the 'species approach' common until that moment in international law. The ecosystem approach is the guiding principle of all programmes of work of the CBD and 'is based on the application of appropriate scientific methodologies focused on levels of biological organization, which encompass the essential structure, processes, functions and interactions among organisms and their environment. It also recognizes that humans, with their cultural diversity, are an integral component of many ecosystems'; see Secretariat of CBD (2004: 1). For a broader view on the landscape approach, see Reed et al. (2016), who define it as a 'framework to integrate policy and practice for multiple competing land uses through the implementation of adaptive and integrated management systems ... [seeking] to address global challenges of poverty alleviation, food security, climate change and biodiversity loss' (2016: 2544).

the recognition of biocultural rights drawing together all of the different rights needed to promote the self-determination and conservation of the cultural identity of a community or people.

Last, but not least, the concept of biocultural rights proposes a way to combine rights and environmental considerations through the balancing of their two foundations. Neither of the two foundations is meant to prevail over the other, and their *coexistence* requires each to be balanced with the other in order to provide for the best possible realization. For example, if a community which was recognized as the holder of biocultural rights guarantees a good conservation of the local ecosystem but not the *best* level of conservation possible—which could otherwise be reached through a typical protected area—such an increase in environmental conservation would not justify the eviction and consequent decrease in the protection of the community's rights. On the contrary, if a community or people revert to unsustainable practices in order to safeguard its traditional rites of passage or the worship of a sacred natural site (a certain rite requires the hunt of a threatened species, once more abundantly present, or to enter an area highly threatened by the very presence of humans), a balance would need to be struck with conservation of the environment.

Biocultural rights have two foundations, and none of the two may be disregarded if we are to remain within their boundaries. The two would have to be balanced, weighed against each other, in the attempt to at least protect both of them partially, thereby limiting their realization to the least possible extent. Biocultural rights are neither purely environmental rights nor are they purely rights of peoples and communities. They are more than engagement in community-based conservation projects—which are aimed at conservation outcomes, counting on mutually beneficial scenarios, and always running the risk of dismissing self-determination, ancestral land occupancy, or cultural rights, if win–win solutions turn out to be unfeasible. Also, they are more than the rights of indigenous peoples and local communities to have their lands and resources protected. They are rights of indigenous peoples and local communities to be stewards of their lands and resources.[10]

Based on these strategic advantages, and given the fact that many indigenous peoples are still struggling to see their indigenous status recognised by their states (Xanthaki 2007: 133), the idea of biocultural rights could provide an alternative—though less favourable—route for the fulfilment of the claims of local communities as well as, in certain circumstances, indigenous peoples.

The next section provides an example which further illustrates what biocultural rights are, how the balancing between rights and conservation may be undertaken, and the strategic advantages they could provide in certain circumstances. The case of the Khwe of Bwabwata National Park is particularly revealing because they are an indigenous people struggling to see its indigenous status recognized by the national government, living within the borders of an imposed national park, maintaining traditional sustainable practices, and asking for rights over their traditional lands and natural resources which

---

[10] Another balancing problem probably coming to the readers' minds concerns the unsustainability of a community action—such as hunting and gathering—and the need for a community to feed itself. This is, however, not a case of conflict between the two foundations of biocultural rights. It is a case of conflict between the second foundation of biocultural rights—conservation of the environment—and other rights of the members of the community: the right to food and right to life. The first foundation of biocultural rights concerns self-determination, land, and cultural rights, not rights to food or to life. The latter two are basic human rights currently granted—though not always enforced—to every human being, regardless of his or her ethnicity, social organization, or sustainable lifestyle. This is therefore a case of conflict between biocultural rights and other community and peoples' rights, which are always considered weightier in any balance of rights, that is, the rights to food and life will always prevail.

are compatible with the objective of the park: conservation of the environment (Bavikatte 2014a).

An Example: Learning from the Khwe[11]

The Khwe of Bwabwata National Park

The beauty of Bwabwata National Park in the Namibian Zambezi Region[12] immediately strikes the visitor a few steps after the entrance gate at the Buffalo check point. Equally striking is the thought of

---

11 The case study is based on literature reviews and data collected during field work conducted in Namibia in 2013 with the non-governmental organization called Natural Justice: Lawyers for Communities and the Environment. The interpretation of the Khwe's case under the light of biocultural rights solely reflects this author's position, not that of Natural Justice. Natural Justice currently is working with the Khwe of Bwabwata National Park, supporting them in the process of creation of a biocultural community protocol (BCP) aimed at requesting the recognition of the rights of the Khwe indigenous peoples, but it is not favourable to the development of the concept of biocultural rights because of some of the dangers explored above. The position of Natural Justice on the topic of biocultural rights can be found in Jonas, Jonas, and Makagon (2014). For more information on the organization, its current and past activities, scope and objectives, see www.naturaljustice.org (accessed 3 January 2018).

12 The Zambezi Region, a long protrusion of about 450 km of Namibian territory that extends towards Zambia and Zimbabwe, and borders Angola and Botswana, was known as the Caprivi Strip until August 2013, when the name was changed as part of the Namibian process of post-independence renaming. The Zambezi Region became part of Namibian territory in 1890, six years after Namibia became a German colony; see Dain-Owens, Kemp, and Lavelle (2010: 1). At the end of World War II, the League of Nations placed Namibia under the control of South Africa until 1966, when the UN declared the occupation illegal.

spending a few days within its borders without a car filled with water, food, and good camping gear.

For the last few hundred years, the indigenous people known as Khwe have lived in those lands, grown and developed their language, culture, and identity, and have survived not only the harshness of the place but also several conflicts with other tribes and different colonial governments. The 12 Khwe communities, composed of about 1,500 members (Legal Assistance Centre 2006: 11), descend from the San, hunter-gatherer indigenous peoples, also known as Bushmen, often described as the first human beings of the world. The San have lived in the area now bordered within Angola, Botswana, Namibia, South Africa, and Zimbabwe for at least 20,000 years, organized in several tribes of nomadic people that called themselves: Ju|'hoansi, Khwe, ||Ani, G|wi, Naro, Hai||om, !Xoò, #Khomani, !Xun, ||Gana, Tshua, ||Xekgwi, and !Ui (Le Roux and White 2004).[13] Each tribe had little contact with the others, but they all shared the same hunter-gatherer livelihoods, a similar click-sound language, traditional dances, and rock art.

Today, approximately 88,000 San remain as 'the most impoverished, disempowered, and stigmatized ethnic group in Southern Africa' (Sylvain 2002: 1074). In Namibia there are about 30,000 San, divided into at least five language groups and located in different areas in the north-east of the country (Legal Assistance Centre 2006: 1). Since the sixteenth century they have been pushed to the fringes of their original territories by Bantu migration from the north (Legal Assistance Centre 2006: 1) and by European colonizers. Today, they are facing problems such as poverty, deprivation of power, and lack of social organization, and mostly live in white-owned farms, or lands owned by other ethnic groups and the government (Legal Assistance Centre 2006: 2–3).

---

[13] The symbols (|, ', !, and #) indicate the different click sounds of the San language.

The resident population of the Zambezi Region consists of approximately 5,000 adults, 82 per cent of whom are San (mostly Khwe) and 18 per cent Mbukushu, a Bantu people that moved to the area about 200 years ago (Dain-Owens, Kemp, and Lavelle 2010: 2). In 1963, a part of the region was proclaimed as the West Caprivi Nature Park (Dain-Owens, Kemp, and Lavelle 2010: 2), and after that, as the Caprivi Game Park in 1968, without any consultation with local residents. In the same year, the refusal of South Africa to grant Namibia independence spawned a war. The Khwe people of the Zambezi Region found themselves involved in military activities, and were forced to leave their territories and reside in army settlements (Boden 2009: 57), as the area was turned into a military zone by the South African Defence Force. When the war ended, and Namibia gained independence in 1990, the Khwe were accused of having collaborated with the South African forces because of their presence in the area and were denied any governmental support (Boden 2008: 115).

In November 2007, the area of the Zambezi Region between the Okawango and the Kwando rivers was proclaimed as the Bwabwata National Park. The park covers an area of 6,274 square km of savanna biome where the Kalahari woodland prevails (Dain-Owens, Kemp, and Lavelle 2010: 8). Any commercial use of land and natural resources within the park needs to be authorized by the Namibian Ministry of Environment and Tourism. The park is divided into different types of areas: the core areas (Mahango, Buffalo, and Kwando)—which have a special level of protection and where settlements, veldt product harvesting, hunting, cattle rearing, and wood collecting are not allowed, and tourism is restricted, and a large multiple-use area—where community-based tourism, trophy hunting, human settlement, plough, and veldt product harvesting are allowed, but limited.

The Khwe communities living in the park mostly rely on natural products for food, building materials, and medicines: they gather veldt products, such as fruits and roots, as well as honey, reeds, grass and wood, and practise very limited small-animal hunting (Dain-Owens, Kemp, and Lavelle 2010). A study of the Round River Conservation Research Centre on the current status of the livelihoods of the Khwe and their impact on the biodiversity in the park recorded the use of 135 plant species as the important food sources for the Khwe and 103 species as the most important for medicinal and cultural purposes (Dain-Owens, Kemp, and Lavelle 2010: 13, 46). The report also revealed that some of the most important alimentary and medicinal plants traditionally used are inaccessible or very scarce in the multiple-use areas (Dain-Owens, Kemp, and Lavelle 2010: 70, 74) and present in higher quantities only in the core areas.

Due to limited access to the core areas of the park, and to the ban on gathering and hunting within those areas, traditional livelihoods are currently not sufficient for the survival of the communities, which therefore increasingly rely on external aid, small jobs, and agriculture (Dain-Owens, Kemp, and Lavelle 2010: 5). Agriculture, however, is strongly restricted because of the lack of water and the negative impact of wildlife on the cultivation of land (elephants, in particular, and no compensation for damaged crops is provided) (Dain-Owens, Kemp, and Lavelle 2010: 59). The ban on hunting and the absence of income necessary to buy meat products (Dain-Owens, Kemp, and Lavelle 2010: 71)[14] (exacerbated by the distance of the very few food stores) worsen the lives of the park's inhabitants, with the result that most lack a balanced diet.

As the representatives of the Khwe emphasized, prohibition to access the core areas is also limiting the ability of the elders to transmit their knowledge and practices about land, animals, and plants to new generations. The Round River study, in fact, reported that 'the new lifestyles have distanced the Khwe from their cultural traditions and

---

[14] In most households the sole source of income are old-age pensions granted by the government for people over 60; see Boden (2008: 115).

led to a loss of local ecological knowledge' (Dain-Owens, Kemp, and Lavelle 2010: 5).

On top of subsistence living and loss of traditional knowledge, life in Bwabwata is hard for the Khwe people due to living alongside the Mbukushu. In the last few years, an increasing number of Mbukushu have settled within the Bwabwata National Park boundaries, bringing along their cattle. It is formally prohibited to import any animal to the park, but they have managed to settle in the multiple-use areas, which, unlike the core areas, are not well-patrolled. Consequently, the Khwe endure not only the legal restrictions on hunting and gathering imposed for conservation purposes, but also the negative consequences of illegal cattle on veldt products.

Khwe life in the park is further complicated by the lack of official recognition granted by the national government. In 1989, the Khwe created a centralized authority but it has not, as yet, received any official recognition as the Khwe Traditional Authority.[15] Many of the Khwe living the park are in fact ruled by Mbukushu leaders, whose traditional authority has received official recognition and which has proclaimed that the Khwe are not a distinct people, but rather, their former subjects (Legal Assistance Centre 2006: 6, 8).

---

[15] According to the Traditional Authorities Act, 2000, traditional authorities can be formed by traditional communities with the following composition: a leader, senior traditional councillors, and traditional councillors elected by the community. Recognized traditional authorities have the power to advise the Namibian president on issues concerning the utilization of communal lands and have the role of ensuring the sustainable use of natural resources and conservation of the environment within communal areas for their own benefit and for the benefit of all Namibians; see Legal Assistance Centre (2006: 13); Ruppel (2008: 113). They decide upon applications for the allocation of customary land rights (rights to farming and residential units) and rights of leasehold; see Communal Land Reform Act, 2002, sections 19 and 20.

The Khwe are sustained in their life within the park by the work of the Namibian non-governmental organization called the Integrated Rural Development and Nature Conservation (IRDNC).[16] One of the IRDNC's most remarkable programmes has been run since 1994 and involves employing 43 Khwe in the management of the park. They act as community game guards and as community resources monitors working inside the park to control wildlife and poaching, to oversee the collection and use of medicinal and food plants, and to advise and teach community members to use sustainable gathering techniques (Taylor 2005). In 2000, the IRDNC helped the Bwabwata residents to create the Kyaramacan Peoples Association, a legal body representing all the residents of the park, of all ethnic groups, on issues concerning the management of natural resources and the distribution of benefits generated from their use.[17]

[16] IRDNC is a non-profit organization that focuses on community-based natural resources management in the Zambesi and Kunene Regions. It is dedicated to wildlife conservation, rural development, and democracy. IRDNC has acted as a bridge between the communities and the government and has worked to establish forms of community-based natural resources management with the Khwe; see Taylor (2005: 37). For more information, visit the IRDNC's official website at: http://www.irdnc.org.na/ (accessed 3 January 2018).

[17] In particular, they are responsible for the distribution of benefits from trophy hunting and the organic harvesting of the devil's claw. The devil's claw, or *Harpagophytum*, has analgesic and anti-inflammatory properties that have long been known by the San and have earned it a place in the European market since the mid-twentieth century; see Cole and Stewart (2005). Until 2007, the park was characterized by large-scale unsustainable and illegal harvesting of devil's claw and their sale for very poor prices. In 2007, with the assistance of the Ministry of Environment and Tourism and IRDNC, the Kyaramacan Peoples Association established a Devil's Claw Management Plan that introduced rules on harvesting methodologies and

'Walk Back to the House of Khwe Traditions'

Strongly concerned about the loss of Khwe's knowledge and practices, and about their struggles to survive, the IRDNC and the Kyaramacan Peoples Association have asked the support of the non-governmental organization, Natural Justice: Lawyers for Communities and the Environment, for the development of a BCP. BCPs are documents resulting from extensive consultations, legal-awareness raising, and community participation, and are aimed at framing the calls of indigenous peoples and local communities within the local, national, and international legal framework (Shrumm and Jonas 2012).[18]

An ad hoc custodians committee, composed of two women and two men elected by the communities, were entitled to lead the Khwe of the park in the development of a BCP aimed at securing rights to access and use of natural resources within Bwabwata's borders. After extensive training on the BCP and consultations with members of the Khwe communities, the committee drafted the Khwe BCP, which describes the relationship of the communities with the natural resources of the park, outlines their specific needs, concerns, and desires, and proposes an alternative configuration of rights and duties within the park. This process is still ongoing (at the time of writing this chapter).

During the first round of consultations, the custodians committee drew the picture of a house with symbols inside and a family outside. They explained that the house represented the culture and knowledge of the Khwe and that the symbols stood for fire, initiation ceremonies (a stick with a drop of blood), the village and its inhabitants, hunting

---

monitoring activities. The association organized trainings for the harvesters, registered them, and obtained the certification of organic products for devil's claw. The income of the harvesters increased three times, and sustainability of the use of resources registered an increase.

[18] For case studies and more publications on BCP, see http://www.community-protocols.org/ (accessed 3 January 2018).

practices (a bow), animals of the park (an animal track), documentation of their traditional knowledge (a book and a pen), and their need to walk back to the house (a human footprint). The family outside the house represented the Khwe of Bwabwata National Park that was outside the house of traditional practices and culture. The family was left out because it could not make fires in the veldt, could not gather the plants its members needed for their food, medicine, and ceremonies, and could not hunt the animals of the park. The last two symbols represented what the family would like to do: record its traditional knowledge in a written form and return to the house of its traditions.

The creation of a written record of their traditional knowledge has begun with the help of IRDNC and would be, as the committee stressed, very useful to teach the Khwe children about their practices. The children mostly went to school and could read; they could not, however, learn the traditional practices of their parents because they spent a lot of time in boarding schools and because they did not have access to those areas of the park where most of animals and plants were. As one of the elders said, 'The children need to see things with their eyes. They should learn to prepare the bow and the arrows, and should go with the hunter to see the footprints, the killing, the lying down animal, and the skinning. But the government is not allowing it anymore.'

The draft BCP reflects the traditional knowledge and practices of the Khwe in line with what the drawing of the house suggested. Most importantly, however, the BCP outlines the request of Bwabwata's Khwe communities to the government, the Ministry of the Environment and Toursim, and the park authorities.

The most pressing element is obtaining special permits to enter the core areas at certain times of the year. The Round River research provides details on the plants, animals, and water sources mostly needed but not available or sufficient in the multiple-use areas and on the seasons and location of each plant species. It was proposed to use it as the source of information to negotiate access rights to the core areas to seasonally collect medicinal plants and food plants unavailable in the multiple-use areas. The Khwe are also asking for recognition of the right to organize periodic trips to the core areas, accompanied by park authorities, to teach younger members of the Khwe about the park. As underlined during the negotiations, Khwe's concern for the transmission of traditional knowledge to new generations is not relevant solely for the communities, their identities, and cultural diversity, but also for the management of the park, as the important role of the community game guards and community resources monitors shows.

Besides access rights and the right to use resources, the Khwe are asking for intervention aimed at improved implementation of park rules. More specifically, they are asking for support in the resolution of conflicts with other tribes living in Bwabwata through the enforcement of the ban on cattle keeping, ending poaching activities, and stopping the cutting of trees in multiple-use areas—a practice the Khwe avoid in accordance with their customary laws.

Overall and most importantly, the Khwe are requesting the recognition of their land and their right to free prior informed consent, in order to mitigate conflicts, stop marginalization, and allow settlements to prosper in peace. Land recognition, they underline, requires the recognition of their traditional authority which would, eventually, work for the implementation of Khwe's customary laws and practices within the park. Moreover, the traditional authority would be accompanied by the custodians committee, charged with providing free prior informed consent on activities on the land and access to their traditional knowledge from outsiders.

The Khwe-Bwabwata case is a clear example of the conflicts that can arise between conservation goals and human rights—in particular rights of indigenous peoples and local communities—which could be resolved with a better understanding of the traditional practices, laws, and world views of the communities and peoples affected. Allowing the Khwe to continue to live, and thrive, within the borders of the park is both a matter of rights to lands and natural resources, to self-government, and to maintain cultural identity, and a matter of conservation of the local environment. The Khwe's requests framed under the label of indigenous rights have not yet been successful with the Namibian government, both because of its attitude towards the Khwe, and because Bwabwata National Park is an environmental conservation hotspot and a source of income from tourism activities over which the government does not want to lose control. The indigenous rights of the Khwe, which should be recognized according to national and international law, have difficult political connotations and are potentially perceived, or labelled, as detrimental for the local environment because they do not encompass environmental responsibilities. The indigenous rights of the Khwe are, in fact, based on the Khwe's indigenous status, not on their conservation role.

Vis-à-vis a state unwilling to abide to international and national law to the point of denying the very indigenous status of the Khwe, a fight for the recognition of indigenous rights is rightful and legitimate, but might be harder to win. In this case, biocultural rights could play an important role, because they could help to overcome the resistance of the government in recognizing the Khwe's indigenous status and rights by placing more importance on the attitude and knowledge of the Khwe towards the environment and their contribution to its conservation. Biocultural rights are not as politically charged as indigenous rights, so claiming them might encounter less tension from the government. Moreover, the sustainability of the Khwe's requests as well as their role as park stewards would be better described under the label of biocultural rights. Biocultural rights present themselves, and their claimants, as environmentally constructed, and ready to find a balance with the conservation of the park.

The Khwe are supporting park authorities, de facto, through their work as community resource monitors and community game guards. Their request for greater access to the park is intended to improve their livelihoods, but also to transmit to their youths that same knowledge needed for the next generation of game guards and resources monitors and to preserve sustainable practices. Besides their knowledge of the park, the Khwe have, through the transmission of traditional knowledge and practices over the last hundreds of years, maintained ways of life that do not require cattle keeping, a practice not compatible with conservation of the park.

At the same time, as a Ministry of the Environment official attending one of the first workshops underlined, 'A hungry people will not refrain, autonomously, from hunting and gathering at an unsustainable level. Limits need to be imposed and enforced from the outside.' This is true, unless there are strong institutional structures in the group that are able to effectively control the action of the members and that are conscious of the consequences of unsustainable uses. The recognition of Khwe's traditional authority, with the support of the Kyaramacan Peoples Association and IRDNC, would certainly work in this direction. The Khwe value the 'Park as a gift of God, to be used as He wishes', and the park and its resources have a paramount significance for their livelihoods and identity. The Khwe's requests show their desire to have secure land recognition (avoiding conflicts with other tribes) and greater access to resources, while at the same time being ready to accept limits for the benefit of the park. They have neither asked to be helped to acquire cattle, nor to be given complete freedom to use park lands and resources, even though the park was created without their consent over their ancestral lands.

What is reported here is just the first round of negotiations and more will be needed to understand how the BCP will develop and what the response of the ministry and the park authorities will be. The requests of the Khwe are intrinsically linked to environmental considerations, because of their own choice and understanding. The biocultural rights framework could turn out to be a very useful tool in their case, which could suggest ways to strike a balance between rights and conservation, a task harder to face when indigenous rights and conservation priorities come into play from two different sides. In such cases, they are two separate bodies of interests and values and one seems to have to come at the expense of the other. Biocultural rights, instead, propose a path towards the balancing of rights and conservation priorities accompanied by mutual support and stewardship relationships.

However, biocultural rights come with a price: the responsibility to promote conservation of the environment. This price might at times be willingly paid as an act of self-determination, at other times it might appear as an unjust burden, especially vis-à-vis the alternative of indigenous rights. But if the alternative of indigenous rights recognition is far and blurred, biocultural rights might be a precious (and sole) alternative.

What really counts is, however, to develop full consciousness of what the concept of biocultural rights entails: namely, considering its potential benefits and disadvantages. Only then can indigenous peoples and local communities decide whether to ask for their recognition or not, always remembering that they are to be handled with care.

6 Past, Present, and Future

Beyond Biocultural Rights

An Appraisal

The idea of biocultural rights appears in international discourse in combination with the new wave of rights-based conservation. Inspired by the ethical theories of indigenous peoples and local communities, biocultural rights come alive—although they are not yet entrenched in law—as a concept which connects international agreements, declarations, treaties, court cases, and laws, and which mainly builds on the assumption that many indigenous peoples and local communities have a special stewardship role towards the environment, and that such stewardship needs the protection of certain rights in order to be maintained.

Biocultural rights derive from the recognition that actions and projects aimed at the conservation of environment have a history of human rights disrespect and abuse when dealing with indigenous peoples and local communities. Technocratic 'fences-and-fines' approaches to conservation have resulted in land evictions, negated use and access to natural resources, and denied self-determination. In the last 30–40 years, rights-based conservation approaches have opened the way to different solutions, promising mutually beneficial scenarios providing care for both the environment and peoples.

According to the construction so far described, the rights to fill the biocultural rights baskets are those necessary to protect the stewardship role of indigenous peoples and local communities and can be divided into four categories: rights to land and resources, rights to self-determination, rights to cultural identity, and procedural rights. In order for such rights to be fulfilled, states, private companies, and international institutions need to abide by corresponding duties, such as allowing indigenous peoples and local communities to live on their traditional lands, guaranteeing access and use of natural resources, seeking free prior informed consent, and guaranteeing the respect of access and benefit sharing provisions.

The environmental genealogy of biocultural rights provides them with a dual foundation based on a heterogeneous combination of protected interests and values: the first foundation lies in the interests of indigenous peoples and local communities in upholding their self-determination and protecting their cultural identity; the second foundation is based on a wider concern, namely, conservation of the environment (which may be interpreted according to both the anthropocentric and non-anthropocentric ethic approaches: as an interest of humankind or as a value per se). This second foundation is also the origin of the sui generis nature of biocultural rights. They are human rights which recognize the importance of self-determination and cultural identity for the survival and flourishing of indigenous peoples and local communities. Nevertheless, they limit these peoples' and communities' interests in order to uphold a general interest: conservation of the environment.

The need to free biocultural rights from considerations and expectations derived from falling into the 'noble savage' myth, which endanger both the protection of the environment and the rights of indigenous peoples and local communities, unveils the important consequences of this sui generis nature. The recognition of the basket of rights mentioned above is not sufficient for guaranteeing the conservation of sustainable practices and lifestyles. Within the biocultural rights framework, the lifestyles and practices of indigenous peoples and local communities would be bound by a duty of sustainability.

The recognition of such a duty raises various problems about the nature of sanctions to enforce the duty, the subjects entitled to claim such enforcement, the standards of environmental protection to be used to judge violations, and, finally, who should be in charge of judging such violations. These problems appear particularly significant vis-à-vis the danger of falling for the 'noble state' myth, granting states more power and trust than they deserve.

Even more importantly, the recognition of a duty to uphold sustainability raises problems concerning whether it is fair to subject biocultural rights to environmental considerations, and to entrust indigenous peoples and local communities with the protection of an interest that actually is held by all of humankind. This question needs to be answered differently for indigenous peoples and local communities. Local communities are not currently recognized as subjects in international law and are only recently being granted rights in conjunction with their role as stewards of biodiversity and ecosystems. Hence, for local communities, biocultural rights could be a strategic concept to be used to argue in favour of the protection of their interests. In contrast, indigenous peoples have a body of hard-fought and recognized indigenous rights which encompass the same favourable legal positions of the biocultural rights basket, but not their environmental duties.

Such a difference in rights recognition does not keep indigenous peoples from being holders of biocultural rights, and this in itself does not infringe their rights. From a legal point of view, there is no reason to believe that indigenous peoples sharing a set of rights with a different subject—in this case local communities—may weaken their legal position. However, political considerations need to be raised, acknowledging that linking the rhetoric on indigenous peoples to their role as stewards of the environment might be dangerous: such a linkage could be used to make indigenous peoples' rights *rhetorically* liable on environmental considerations and sustainable lifestyles a precondition for their recognition.

Besides the points of critique, it must be underlined that biocultural rights—with the needed attention—could, if recognized, be strategically useful for indigenous peoples whose indigenous status or rights are denied, as is the case with the Khwe people of Bwabwata National Park. Biocultural rights could be used as an instrument to obtain rights in cases in which claims of indigenous rights are not successful (because a state denies the existence of an indigenous people or favours the creation of a protected area over the fulfilment of indigenous rights, for example). Biocultural rights could in fact appear more politically neutral for states unwilling to comply with international law because they fear indigenous self-determination or need to face critical environmental challenges. They can, therefore, represent a second (although less appealing) option for indigenous peoples to get their interests protected. Moreover, a 'biocultural rights landscape' approach could provide a comprehensive basket to address all the relevant rights needed by a community or people to maintain its lands, resources, and lifestyles, without having to revert to many different fora and pieces of legislation (for example, access and benefit sharing, water rights, intellectual property rights, or right to freedom of religion).

Overall, the idea of biocultural rights could prove strategically useful for local communities and, in fewer cases, for indigenous peoples. They should, however, be fully understood before being claimed, in order to place each community and people in the best possible condition to decide whether they want to take the route of biocultural rights or not.

Moving beyond strategic and political considerations, a further point deserves some attention. The development of the concept of biocultural rights—it seems to this author—could provide some hints to counter the wider problem concerning the difficult equilibrium between human rights and protection of the environment in the Anthropocene.

Human Rights in the Anthropocene

What do human rights look like in a very crowded, damaged world? Are they different, or supposed to be different? Human rights had been conceived as suitable and appropriate to address the needs of human beings in a world that had not entered the Anthropocene. It was a world human beings could not damage or overuse to the point of ruining it forever. At that time, nature and environmental resources were *taken for granted*. They were not factored into the human rights discourse as limited assets, because *taking* could be increased unlimitedly (Bosselmann 2015: 535). There was no knowledge about the upcoming environmental crisis, as, unfortunately, there still is too little.

Most of traditional human rights theory and rhetoric are still characterized by an 'ecological blindness' (Taylor 1998: 314). They focus on the realization of human needs and the regulation of relationships between individuals, society, and the state, and only timidly acknowledge the link between humans and the surrounding environment (Taylor 1998: 314). Human rights theory understands nature as either a 'storehouse of raw materials' to be used to satisfy human needs or as an object of fear from which humans are to be protected (Taylor 2008: 93). Human rights seem to exist in a *vacuum*, not within the natural world (Taylor 2008: 93).

Human rights are in fact an instrument aimed at protecting human interests. Even if understood in a broad sense—for example, by embracing environmental rights, such as the right to enjoy a beautiful and healthy environment—human rights theory especially focuses on securing those interests of human beings that are considered crucial for preserving human intrinsic value. Therefore, they make individuals, or groups of individuals, the centre of the discussion where they are the addressee of someone else's duty, typically the state, other individuals, or communities. Human beings are turned into receivers of goods and services because human rights were conceived to protect them from the paramount power of states and lords. These interests are secured by placing them above general interests or values, including the protection of the environment. Consequently, in this anthropocentric approach, the protection of the environment may always be overridden by human rights considerations.[1]

Vis-à-vis the current environmental crisis, the relationship between human rights and the environment is increasingly problematic. The entrance into the Anthropocene, either as a metaphor or as a proper geological era, requires us to better understand and find alternative solutions to the need to uphold human rights while at the same time protecting the environment. If we do not find these solutions we will see the very legitimacy of human rights weakened: '[W]ithout the recognition of their ecological embeddedness and addressing the ecological crises, human rights may undermine their own material basis and lose their legitimacy in discourses concerning justice' (Fisher and Lundberg 2015: 181). As inequalities, violence, and genocides have not been erased from the planet, we are very much in need of preserving human rights and their legitimacy. In order to do so, the human rights rhetoric—not only politics—needs to make friends with natural sciences and work together to tackle the environmental crisis.

[1] As Bosselmann (2015: 531) notes, human rights and protection of the environment have different 'underpinning rationalities and human welfare is considered superior to the environment under the current international human rights regime'.

The ability of a population of lions to drive a population, or even a species, of gazelles to extinction, cannot be compared to the power of human beings to harm their natural environments. We have managed to obtain a power to change ecosystems that goes beyond that of any other species, and we have expanded our population beyond the environmental carrying capacity of the earth. The attitude of asking, of pretending, of being a mere addressee may be comprehensible if the counterpart is a state. But if the counterpart is the environment, our attitude has to be different. Human rights rhetoric cannot be deaf to these considerations, it needs to be adjusted.

The first thing that comes to mind is a change in the underpinning ethics of human rights—a change in what we accord intrinsic value to, in the hierarchies of values to which we refer. For example, Bosselmann (2008: 121–31) suggests that it is not enough to adapt the human rights rhetoric to the current environmental challenges because human rights are part of that same anthropocentric system that led us to such a crisis. He (2015: 549) suggests the incorporation of the idea of duties and responsibilities based on 'ecological limitations' and calls for the creation of a 'theory on how environmental human rights may be complemented by environmental duties'.

The adoption of non-anthropocentric ethics, the recognition of moral standing of animals, plants, entire species, or the earth are attempts to shift the focus away from human beings, either bringing other natural entities into the realm of rights (animal rights theories) or granting value to whole ecosystems. However, while animal rights theories are not always compatible with conservation considerations, ecocentric ethics still encounter strong critique, including the accusations of *environmental fascism* and naturalistic fallacy.

Biocultural rights suggest a different route. Rather than entering the shifting grounds of gigantic changes in ethical paradigms, they allow us to maintain the focus on human rights and interests. The interest in conservation of the environment can be framed as an interest of humankind (including future generations if its scope is to be widened), or as a value per se. This allows us to shift from an anthropocentric to a non-anthropocentric approach, depending on the one we see as more applicable, useful, or effective. For example, when talking to politicians and governments, an anthropocentric approach might be more effective, comprehensible, and acceptable for voters. This approach would allow conservation of the environment to gain a privileged position within the human rights discourse, without, necessarily, waiting for human psychology (as Aldo Leopold [1949] hopes) to value the environment *regardless of* human beings.

Within the biocultural rights structure, duties can be incorporated not simply as external restrictions, but as inherent foundations. The very reason why a certain biocultural rights basket is conferred is not only the interest of the right holder but also an interest in conservation of the environment. Balancing human rights and the environment is an intrinsic characteristic of biocultural rights. The claim for biocultural rights is in itself the acceptance of the importance that certain indigenous peoples and local communities attach to conservation. Biocultural rights are, by definition, a combination of human interests and environmental values.

A Local Communities Proposal

When elaborating further on the subject, one question seems to be inevitable. Why should biocultural rights, in search of a balance between human rights and protection of the environment, be only applied to indigenous peoples and local communities—precisely those subjects recognized as less detrimental for conservation? In a world undergoing an environmental crisis, no human right, except for very basic human rights, should be detached from environmental considerations.

However, the very nature of biocultural rights as *human* rights has revealed to be their most problematic feature. Conditioning a set of human rights of indigenous peoples and local communities—protecting very important interests and needs—to environmental considerations has given rise to the problems underlined in Chapters 4 and 5. This is precisely because it is dangerous to limit a set of human rights to considerations relevant for the general interest or the protection of a value per se—even if it is as important as conservation of the environment. For this reason, future research on biocultural rights could, rather than dismissing biocultural rights because of their potentially unfair implications for indigenous peoples, shift the focus towards local communities, enlarging their conceptual scope to also incorporate non-traditional communities, and concentrating on a set of rights which do not necessarily qualify as human rights.

According to Bavikatte and Bennett (2015: 28), '[W]hile, for the most part, biocultural rights are associated with communities that have strong cultural and spiritual ties to their lands, there is no reason why they should not also be claimed by urban communities aspiring to protect the destruction of their parks, wetlands, lakes and trees in the name of development.' Such a focus may lead to expand the discourse of *biocultural diversity*, as Cocks (2006: 190) suggests, to include also less 'exotic' communities that have migrated to peri-urban or urban areas and that have maintained a 'nature-related sense of cultural identity' (2006: 191, 195). She argues that a community does not need to 'live geographically close to natural environment for it to hold spiritual, social, and cultural value' (2006: 194) and that the theory of 'biocultural diversity' should also include more varied social groups (2006: 195). Those communities that live in urban or peri-urban areas may be holders of very important ecological knowledge concerning medicinal and other uses of plants and animals parts, and may attach spiritual or religious values to such practices and species.

In the discourse about further developed biocultural rights, local communities may be traditional, 'such as small-scale farmers, artisanal fishing communities, island and mountain communities—that do not fit the strict test of indigeneity but nevertheless have tradition-ally maintained a lifestyle and socio-economic practices as well as knowledge and value systems, which are intimately connected to land

and nature' (Bessa 2015: 332), or non-traditional—communities of mainstream religions worshipping and protecting sacred natural sites, such as streams, shores, mountains (Frascaroli et al. 2015; Mallarach 2012; Mallarach and Papayannis 2010: 203; Wild 2010); communities which have preserved certain pastoralist and agricultural practices contributing to the conservation of genetic resources of local varieties; newly established communities voluntarily detaching themselves from mainstream society with the precise aim to live sustainably and create ecovillages (Ergas 2010: 34);[2] or groups of citizens who claim for the possibility to manage and care for a natural area (which may be a urban park, a shore, or a watercourse).

All these communities, which have maintained or created a special link with certain lands and natural resources, may be capable of exercising a stewardship role towards the local environment if they are granted certain rights. These rights may be property rights (commons, civic usages of state lands), intellectual property rights over genetic resources (farmers' privileges, pastoralists' rights, fair and equitable benefit sharing), or a certain level of self-government rights. Since each community or people will have different needs in terms of rights to maintain their way of life, the rights will necessarily vary from one context to another in response to local circumstances. And, most importantly, such biocultural rights would be based on two concurring foundations: the special link with a certain territory and the commitment to conservation of the environment.

These communities would be conferred not only a basket of rights, but also a set of environmental duties. Such a duty of stewardship towards the environment would compensate all other inhabitants of

[2] According to the Global Ecovillage Network, 'An ecovillage is an intentional or traditional community that is consciously designed through locally owned, participatory processes to regenerate social and natural environments. The four dimensions of sustainability (ecology, economy, the social and the cultural) are all integrated into a holistic approach'; see Kunze and Avelino (2015: 6).

the country—which remain excluded from those lands and resources—for the special rights such communities would receive. Other citizens would benefit from the attribution of such special rights because those local communities would support the protection of the environment, which is a cost for states.

Further research is necessary to explore and understand the content of such a duty of sustainability. It should be surely higher than a general duty of abiding with national and international environmental law, but how much higher? Is there a standard of conservation beyond which the duty of stewardship would become an 'unfair' burden for the right holders? Who would be entitled to determine the standard of conservation required? Moreover, questions would emerge concerning sanctions over the withdrawal of the right, the body entrusted with determining these sanctions, and the potentially unfair implications stemming from their enforcement.

These re-envisioned biocultural rights would have, of course, a limited impact on global pollution and environmental degradation; however, they would respond to the repeatedly cited Principle 19 of the Stockholm Declaration,[3] calling on individuals and communities

---

[3] The Stockholm Declaration was adopted in 1972 at the United Nations Conference on Human Environment. The Declaration, though a non-binding document, represented a milestone in the evolution of international environmental law and a great catalyst for the adoption of future binding multilateral environmental agreements. The Declaration includes a Preamble and 26 Principles among which the right to a healthy environment, the responsibility to protect the environment for present and future generations, and the principle of cooperation among states to achieve the best possible protection of the environment, and a call for 'the younger generation as well as adults, giving due consideration to the underprivileged, ... [as] essential in order to broaden the basis for an enlightened opinion and responsible conduct by individuals, enterprises and communities in protecting and improving the environment in its full human dimension'.

to protect and improve the environment in its full human dimension. It would also be an attempt to undertake environmental responsibilities not only in developing countries—as conservation practices mostly do—but also in rich, technology-advanced ones and to guide their citizens, including groups of urban residents, to change their impact on the earth.

A word of caution is needed, however. Such re-envisioned biocultural rights could act as a set of rights, and duties, which add to the current body of rights and human rights, but would not substitute them: biocultural rights would not replace local communities' human rights (as they do not substitute indigenous rights in the original construction by Bavikatte). They would, rather, add to the already existing bodies of rights. In particular, they should not be confused or merged with human rights. The further step of conditioning human rights with environmental considerations still requires challenging and deeply engaged research and should be faced with much caution to avoid dangerous implications. For example, it would be extremely risky to conceive an environmentally limited right to freedom of thought and expression. To add to the foundations of the right to freedom of thought and expression the protection of the environment would compel thought and expression to be beneficial for the protection of the environment. This could, for instance, vis-à-vis strong scientific disagreements, lead to compare theses with allegedly anti-environmental implications to *negationist* positions (Latour 2015), thus de facto threatening freedom of research.

All new ideas need to be researched, thought through, and digested, before concluding that they are good ideas. Some may be good vessels to safely reach the other side of the ocean, others may be not. None is a panacea. All must be looked at with circumspection, open eyes, and an open mind. Throughout this book, the attempt has been to draw attention to some aspects, positive and negative, of the concept of biocultural rights. The book would have achieved what it set out to do if the reader now feels that they know a bit more about what biocultural rights are, what they might be used for, what their dangers are, and how they might evolve, changing their status and welcoming new holders. Final decisions, such as whether or not to use biocultural rights, rest with the affected peoples and communities. They are the real judges, not the academics. This book attempted to provide intellectual resources; their right is to use them as they like.

Bibliography

Adams, Daglas N. 1979. *Hitchhikers' Guide to the Galaxy*. London: Pan Books.

Adams, William M. 2003. 'Nature and the Colonial Mind', in Williams M. Adams and Martin Mulligan (eds), *Decolonizing Nature: Strategies for Conservation in a Post-Colonial Era*, pp. 16–50. London, Sterling, VA: Earthscan.

Adams, William M., and Martin Milligan (eds). 2003. *Decolonizing Nature. Strategies for Conservation in a Post-Colonial Era*. London, Sterling, VA: Earthscan.

Agrawal, Arun, and Clark C. Gibson. 1999. 'Enchantment and Disenchantment: The Role of Community in Natural Resource Conservation', *World Development*, 27(4): 629–49.

Agrawal, Arun, Daniel Nepstad, and Ashwini Chhatre. 2011. 'Reducing Emissions from Deforestation and Forest Degradation'. *Annual Review of Environment and Resources*, 36: 373–96.

Alcorn, Janis. 1993. 'Indigenous Peoples and Conservation'. *Conservation Biology*, 7(2): 424–6.

———. 2008. 'Beauty and the Beast: Human Rights and Biocultural Diversity'. *Resurgence Magazine*, September: 250.

Anaya, James. 1996. *Indigenous Peoples in International Law*. Oxford: Oxford University Press.

Anaya, James. 1997. 'On Justifying Special Ethnic Group Rights: Comments on Pogge'. In Ian Shapiro and Will Kymlicka (eds), *Ethnicity and Group Rights*, pp. 222–31. New York, London: New York University Press.

Antkowiak, Thomas M. 2007. 'Moiwana Village v. Suriname: A Portal into Recent Jurisprudential Developments of the Inter-American Court of Human Rights', *Berkeley Journal of International Law*, 25(2): 268–82.

Banner, Stuart. 2005. 'Why *Terra Nullius?* Anthropology and Property Law in Early Australia', *Law and History Review*, 23(1): 95–131.

Barbujani, Guido. 2005. 'Human Races: Classifying People vs Understanding Diversity'. *Current Genomics*, 6(4): 215–26.

Barnosky, Anthony D., Nicholas Matzke, Susumu Tomiya, Guinevere O.U. Wogan, Brian Swartz, Tiago B. Quental, Charles Marshall, et al. 2011. 'Has the Earth's Sixth Mass Extinction Already Arrived?', *Nature*, 471: 51–7.

Barsh, Russel Lawrence. 1995. 'Indigenous Peoples and the Idea of Human Rights', *Native Studies Review*, 10(2): 35–55.

Bavikatte, Sanjay Kabir. 2012. 'Stewarding the Commons: Rethinking Property and the Emergence of Biocultural Rights', *Common Voices*, 7: 20–25.

———. 2014. *Stewarding the Earth. Rethinking Property and the Emergence of Biocultural Rights*. New Delhi: Oxford University Press.

———. 2014a. 'Biocultural Community Protocols and the Future of Conservation', *OUPblog*, 8 September. Available online at http://blog.oup.com/2014/09/biocultural-community-protocols-future-conservation/ (last accessed on 19 February 2017).

Bavikatte, Sanjay Kabir, and Daniel Robinson. 2011. 'Towards a People's History of the Law: Biocultural Jurisprudence and the Nagoya Protocol on Access and Benefit Sharing', *Law Environment and Development*, 7(1): 35–51.

Bavikatte, Sanjay Kabir, and Tom Bennett. 2015. 'Community Stewardship: The Foundation of Biocultural Rights', *Journal of Human Rights and the Environment*, 6(1): 7–29.

Baxi, Upendra. 2002. *The Future of Human Rights*. New Delhi: Oxford University Press.

Becker, C. Dustin, and Elinor Ostrom. 1995. 'Human Ecology and Resource Sustainability: The Importance of Institutional Diversity', *Annual Review of Ecology and Systematics*, 26: 113–33.

Beitz, Charles R. 2001. 'Human Rights as a Common Concern', *The American Political Science Review*, 95(2): 269–82.

———. 2003. 'What Human Rights Mean', *Daedalus*, 132(1): 36–46.

Bèlair, C., K. Ichikawa, B.Y.L. Wong, and K.J. Mulongoy (eds). 2010. *Sustainable Use of Biological Diversity in Socio-Ecological Production Landscapes: Background to the 'Sotoyama Initiative for the Benefit of Biodiversity and Human Well-Being'*. Montreal: Secretariat of the Convention on Biological Diversity.

Benson, John. 2000. *Environmental Ethics: An Introduction with Readings*. London, New York: Routledge.

Berkes, Fikret. 2004. 'Rethinking Community-Based Conservation', *Conservation Biology*, 18(3): 621–30.

Bessa, Adriana. 2015. 'Traditional Local Communities: What Lessons Can Be Learnt at the International Level from the Experiences of Brazil and Scotland?' *Review of European, Comparative & International Environmental Law*, 24(3): 330–40.

Bloch, Anne-Christine. 2001. 'Minorities and Indigenous Peoples', in Asbjørn Eide, Catarina Krause, and Allan Rosas (eds), *Economic, Social and Cultural Rights*, pp. 373–88. Dordrecht, Boston, London: Martinus Nijhoff Publishers.

Bobbio, Norberto. 1988. 'Il Primato Dei Diritti Sui Doveri' ('The Primacy of Rights on Duties'), in M. Bovero *Teoria Generale Della Politica* (*General Theory of Politics*), pp. 431–40. Torino, Italy: Einaudi. English edition, *The Age of Rights*, translated by Allan Cameron, published in 1996 by Polity Press, Cambridge.

Boden, Gertrud. 2008. '"The Young People Do What They Want": Negotiating Inter-Generational Relationships among the Khwe of Namibia', in Erdmute Alber, Sjaak van der Geest, and Susan Reynolds Whyte (eds), *Generations in Africa: Connections and Conflicts*, pp. 113–35. Münster: Lit Verlag.

————. 2009. 'The Khwe and West Caprivi before Namibian Independence: Matters of Land, Labour, Power and Alliance', *Journal of Namibian Studies*, 5: 27–71.

Borrini-Feyerabend, Grazia, Ashish Kothari, and Gonzalo Oviedo (eds). 2004. *Indigenous and Local Communities and Protected Areas. Towards Equity and Enhanced Conservation. Best Practice Protected Area Guidelines Series No. 11*. World Commission on Protected Areas (WCPA). Available at http://pubs.iied.org/G02786/ (accessed 3 January 2018).

Bosselmann, Klaus. 2008. *The Principle of Sustainability. Transforming Law and Governance*. Aldershot, Burlington: Ashgate.

————. 2015. 'Environmental and Human Rights in Ethical Context', in Anna Grear and Louis J Kotzè (eds), *Research Handbook on Human Rights and the Environment*, pp. 531–49. Cheltenham, Northampton: Edward Elgar Publishing.

Boyd, David R. 2012. *The Environmental Rights Revolution. A Global Study of Constitutions, Human Rights and the Environment*. Vancouver: University of British Columbia Press.

Boyle, Alan. 2012. 'Human Rights and the Environment: Where Next?', *European Journal of International Law*, 23(3): 613–42.

Brechin, Steven R., Peter R. Wilshusen, Crystal L. Fortwangler, and Patrick C. West. 2002. 'Beyond the Square Wheel: Toward a More Comprehensive Understanding of Biodiversity Conservation as Social and Political Process', *Society and Natural Resources*, 15: 41–64.

Brosius, J.P., and D. Russell. 'Conservation from Above: An Anthropological Perspective on Transboundary Protected Areas', *Journal of Sustainable Forestry*, 17(1): 39–65.

Callicott, J. Baird. 1990. 'The Case against Moral Pluralism', *Environmental Ethics*, Summer: 99–124.

———. 1997. 'The Challenge of a World Environmental Ethic', *American Journal of Theology & Philosophy*, 18(1): 65–79.

Cambridge University Press. 2017. 'Catch-22', *Cambridge Dictionary*. Available at https://dictionary.cambridge.org/ (accessed 3 January 2018).

Campese, Jessica. 2009. 'Rights-Based Approaches to Conservation: An Overview of Concepts and Questions', in Jessica Campese, Terry Sunderland, Thomas Greiber, and Gonzalo Oviedo (eds), *Rights-Based Approaches: Exploring Issues and Opportunities for Conservation*, pp. 1–45. Bogor: IUCN and IFOR.

Cavalli-Sforza, Luca, Paolo Menozzi, and Alberto Piazza. 1994. *The History and Geography of Human Genes*. Princeton, NJ: Princeton University Press.

CBD. 2014. XII/12: Article 8(j) and Related Provisions; Vol. UNEP/CBD/C. Pyeongchang.

Ceballos, Gerardo, Paul R. Ehrlich, Anthony D. Barnosky, Andrés García, Robert M. Pringle, and Todd M. Palmer. 2015. 'Accelerated Modern Human-Induced Species Losses: Entering the Sixth Mass Extinction', *Science Advances*, 1: 1–5.

Chandra, Rajshree. 2016a. 'Understanding Change With(in) Law: The Niyamgiri Case', *Contributions to Indian Sociology*, 50(2): 137–62.

———. 2016b. *The Cunning of Rights: Law, Life, Biocultures*. Oxford: Oxford University Press.

Chelazzi, Guido. 2013. *L'impronta Originale: Storia Naturale Della Colpa Ecologica (The Original Footprint: Natural History of the Ecological Fault)*. Torino: Einaudi.

Claus, Anne C., Chan M.A. Kai, and Terre Satterfield. 2010. 'The Roles of People in Conservation', in Navjot S. Sodhi and Paul R. Ehrlich (eds), *Conservation Biology for All*, pp. 262–83. Oxford: Oxford University Press.

Cocks, Michelle. 2006. 'Biocultural Diversity: Moving Beyond the Realm of "Indigenous" and "Local" People', *Human Ecology*, 34(2): 185–200.

Cole, D., and M. Stewart. 2005. 'The Commercial Harvest of Devil's Claw (Harpagophytum Spp.) in Southern Africa: The Devil's in the Details', *Journal of Ethnopharmacology*, 100(3): 225–36.

Crawfurd, John. 1861. 'On the Conditions Which Favour, Retard, or Obstruct the Early Civilization of Man', *Transactions of the Ethnological Society of London*, 1: 154–77.

Cullinan, Cormac. 2002. *Wild Law*. Cape Town, South Africa: Siber Ink.

Dain-Owens, Susie, Lucy Kemp, and Jessica Lavelle. 2010. *An Assessment of Plant Resource Use and Its Role in Food Security for Communities Living within Bwabwata National Park, West Caprivi*. Salt Lake City.

Daniels, Brigham. 'Emerging Commons and Tragic Institutions', *Environmental Law*, 37: 515–71.

DesJardins, Joseph R. 2013. *Environmental Ethics: An Introduction to Environmental Philosophy*. Belmont, California: Wadsworth Cengage Learning.

Deveaux, Monique. 2000.'Conflicting Equalities? Cultural Group Rights and Sex Equality', *Political Studies*, 48: 522–39.

Diamond, Jared. 1997. *Guns, Germs, and Steel: The Fates of Human Societies*. New York, London: W.W. Norton & Company.

———. 2005. *Collapse: How Societies Choose to Fail or Succeed*. New York: Penguin Group.

Dutfield, Graham. 1999. 'Rights, Resources and Responses', in Darrell Addison Posey (ed.), *Cultural and Spiritual Values of Biodiversity. A Complementary Contribution to the Global Biodiversity Assessment*, pp. 503–50. Nairobi: Intermediate Technology Publication.

Dworkin, Ronald. 1978.'Taking Rights Seriously', in *Taking Rights Seriously*, pp. 184–205. Cambridge, MA: Harvard University Press.

———. 1984.'Rights as Trumps', in Jeremy Waldron (ed.), *Theories of Rights*, pp. 153–67. Oxford: Oxford University Press.

———. 1977. *Taking Rights Seriously*. Cambridge, MA: Harvard University Press.

Ellingson, Ter. 2001. *The Myth of the Noble Savage*. London: University of California Press.

Ergas, Christina. 2010.'A Model of Sustainable Living: Collective Identity in an Urban Ecovillage', *Organization & Environment*, 23(1): 32–54.

FAO. 1989. 'Proceedings of the Twenty-Fifth Session of the FAO Conference', Rome, 11–29 November.

Ferraris, Luchino, and Cath Traynor. 2016.'The Binding Nature of the 2015 Paris Agreement & Outcomes for Indigenous Peoples and Local Communities. Report by Natural Justice. Available at http://naturaljustice.org/publication/the-binding-nature-of-the-2015-paris-agreement-outcomes-for-indigenous-peoples-and-local-communities/ (accessed 3 January 2018).

Fisher, Aled Dilwyn, and Maria Lundberg. 2015.'Human Rights' Legitimacy in the Face of the Global Ecological Crisis: Indigenous Peoples, Ecological

Rights Claims and the Inter-American Human Rights System', *Journal of Human Rights and the Environment*, 6(2): 177–203.

Forest People Programme. 2011. *Case Studies and Synthesis Paper on Customary Sustainable Use of Biodiversity by Indigenous Peoples and Local Communities: Examples, Challenges, Community Initiatives and Recommendations Relating to CBD Article 10(c)*. Forest People Programme. Available at http://www.forestpeoples.org/sites/fpp/files/publication/2010/10/10c-synthesisfp-poct10loresen.pdf (accessed 3 January 2018).

Francioni, Francesco. 2010.'International Human Rights in an Environmental Horizon', *European Journal of International Law*, 21(1): 41–55.

Frascaroli, Fabrizio, Shonil Bhagwat, Riccardo Guarino, Alessandro Chiarucci, and Bernhard Schmid. 2015.'Shrines in Central Italy Conserve Plant Diversity and Large Trees', *Ambio*, 45(4): 468–79.

Gavin, Michael C., Joe McCarter, Aroha Mead, Fikret Berkes, John Richard Stepp, Debora Peterson, and Ruifei Tang. 2015. 'Defining Biocultural Approaches to Conservation', *Trends in Ecology and Evolution*, 30(3): 140–5.

Gearty, Conor. 2010. 'Do Human Rights Help or Hinder Environmental Protection?', *Journal of Human Rights and the Environment*, 1(1): 7–22.

Global Witness. 2015. *On Dangerous Ground: 2015's Deadly Environment: The Killing and Criminalization of Land and Environmental Defenders Worldwide*. London: Global Witness.

Godden, Lee, and Maureen Tehan. 2016. 'REDD+: Climate Justice and Indigenous and Local Community Rights in an Era of Climate Disruption', *Journal of Energy & Natural Resources Law*, 34(1): 95–108.

Grant, Evadne. 2015.'International Human Rights Courts and Environmental Human Rights: Re-Imagining Adjudicative Paradigms', *Journal of Human Rights and the Environment*, 6(2): 156–76.

Gray, Andrew. 1999. 'Indigenous Peoples, Their Environments and Territories', in Darrell Addison Posey (ed.), *Cultural and Spiritual Values of Biodiversity. A Complementary Contribution to the Global Biodiversity Assessment*, pp. 59–118. Nairobi: Intermediate Technology Publication.

Greiber, Thomas (ed.). 2009. *Conservation with Justice: A Rights-Based Approach*. Gland, Switzerland: IUCN.

Greiber, Thomas, Sonia Moreno Peña, Mattias Åhrén, Jimena Nieto Carrasco, Evanson Chege Kamau, Jorge Medaglia Cabrera, Maria Julia Oliva, Frederic Perron-Welch, China Williams, and Natasha Ali (eds). 2012. *An Explanatory Guide to the Nagoya Protocol on Access and Benefit-Sharing: IUCN Environmental Policy and Law Paper No. 83*. Gland, Switzerland: IUCN.

Griffin, James. 2008. *On Human Rights.* Oxford: Oxford University Press.

Grove, Richard H. 1995. *Green Imperialism: Colonial Expansion, Tropical Island Edens and the Origins of Environmentalism, 1600–1800.* Cambridge: Cambridge University Press.

Hamilton, Clive, Christophe Bonneuil, and Francois Gemenne. 2015. 'Thinking the Anthropocene', in Clive Hamilton, Christophe Bonneuil, and Francois Gemenne (eds), *The Anthropocene and the Global Environmental Crisis: Rethinking Modernity in a New Epoch,* pp. 1–13. London, New York: Earthscan, Routledge.

Hardin, Garrett. 1968. 'The Tragedy of the Commons', *Science,* 162: 1243–50.

Hart, Herbert Lionel Adolphus. 1982. 'Legal Rights', in *Essays on Bentham: Studies in Jurisprudence and Political Theory,* pp. 162–93. Oxford: Clarendon Press.

Hartney, Michael. 1995. 'Some Confusions Concerning Collective Rights', in Will Kymlicka (ed.), *The Rights of Minority Cultures,* pp. 202–27. Oxford: Oxford University Press.

Hingston, Richard W.G. 1931. 'Proposed British National Parks for Africa', *Geographical Journal,* 77: 401–28.

Hohfeld, Wesley N. 1919. 'Fundamental Legal Conceptions, I and II', in Wheeler W. Cook (ed.), *Some Fundamental Legal Conceptions as Applied in Judicial Reasoning.* New Haven: Yale University Press.

Hsiao, Elaine. 2012. 'Whanganui River Agreement: Indigenous Rights and Rights of Nature', *Environmental Policy and Law,* 42(6): 371–5.

Iorns Magallanes, Catherine J. 2015. 'Nature as an Ancestor: Two Examples of Legal Personality for Nature in New Zealand', *VertigO: La Revue Électronique En Sciences de L'environnement,* 1–16.

IUCN. 2016. 'IUCN Programme 2017–2020'. Available online at https://portals.iucn.org/library/sites/library/files/documents/WCC-6th-001.pdf (last accessed on 19 February 2017).

Jacoby, Karl. 2001. *Crimes against Nature: Squatters, Poachers, Thieves, and the Hidden History of American Conservation.* Berkeley, Los Angeles, London: University of California Press.

Jaksa, Matthew F. 2006. 'Putting the "Sustainable" Back in Sustainable Development: Recognizing and Enforcing Indigenous Property Rights as a Pathway to Global Environmental Sustainability', *Journal of Environmental Law and Litigation,* 21(1): 157–206.

Jodoin, Sébastien. 2016. 'The Human Rights of Indigenous Peoples and Forest-Dependent Communities in the Complex Legal Framework for REDD+', in Christina Voigt (ed.), *Research Handbook on REDD+ and International Law,* pp. 157–85. London: Edward Elgar Press, 2016.

Johnston, Darlene M. 1995. 'Native Rights as Collective Rights: A Question of Group Self-Preservation', in Will Kymlicka (ed.), *The Rights of Minority Cultures*, pp. 179–201. Oxford: Oxford University Press.

Jonas, Hans (trans. from German by Hans Jonas). 1984 [1979]. *The Imperative of Responsibility*. Chicago: Chicago University Press.

Jonas, Harry, and Holly Shrumm. 2012. *Recalling Traditional Resource Rights: An Integrated Rights Approach to Biocultural Diversity*. Malaysia: Natural Justice.

Jonas, Harry, Eli J. Makagon, and Holly Shrumm. 2013. *The Living Convention: A Compendium of Internationally Recognised Rights That Support the Integrity and Resilience of Indigenous Peoples' and Local Communities' Territories and Other Social-Ecological Systems*. Natural Justice. Available at http://naturaljustice.org/publication/the-living-convention/ (accessed 3 January 2018).

Jonas, Harry, Eli J. Makagon, Stephanie Booker, and Holly Shrumm. 2012. *An Analysis of International Law, National Legislation, Judgements, and Institutions as They Interrelate with Territories and Areas Conserved by Indigenous Peoples and Local Communities*. Bangalore, Pune, Delhi: Natural Justice and Kalpavriksh.

Jonas, Harry, Holly Jonas, and J. Eli Makagon. 2014. 'Introducing the Living Convention and the Landscape Approach to Legal Empowerment', in Wilton Littlechild, and Elsa Stamatopoulou (eds), *Indigenous Peoples' Access to Justice, Including Truth and Reconciliation Processes*, pp. 390–406. New York: Columbia University, Institute for the Study of Human Rights.

Jonas, Harry, Jael Makagon, and Dilys Roe. 2016. 'Conservation Standards: From Rights to Responsibilities', *IIED Discussion Paper*. London.

Jonas, Holly, Harry Jonas, and Suneetha M. Subramanian (eds). 2013. *The Right to Responsibility: Resisting and Engaging Development, Conservation, and the Law in Asia*. Malaysia: Natural Justice and United Nations University—Institute of Advanced Studies.

Jones, Peter. 2014. 'Group Rights', in Edward N. Zalta (ed.), *The Stanford Encyclopaedia of Philosophy*. Available at https://plato.stanford.edu/entries/rights-group/ (accessed 3 January 2018).

Kothari, Ashish, Colleen Corrigan, Harry Jonas, Aurélie Neumann, and Holly Shrumm (eds). 2012. *Recognising and Supporting Territories and Areas Conserved by Indigenous Peoples and Local Communities: Global Overview and National Case Studies*. Montreal: Secretariat of CBD.

Kunze, Iris, and Flor Avelino. 2015. *Social Innovation and the Global Ecovillage Network: Research Report*. Grant agreement no. 613169.

Kuokkanen, Rauna. 2012. 'Self-Determination and Indigenous Women's Rights at the Intersection of International Human Rights', *Human Rights Quarterly*, 34(1): 225–50.

Kymlicka, Will. 1994. 'Individual and Community Rights', in Judith Baker (ed.), *Group Rights*, pp. 17–33. Toronto: University of Toronto Press.

———— (ed.). 1995. *The Rights of Minority Cultures*. Oxford: Oxford University Press.

Laird, Sarah A., and Rachel Wynberg. 2008. *Access and Benefit-Sharing in Practice: Trends in Partnerships across Sectors*. Montreal: Secretariat of CBD.

Latour, Bruno. 2015. 'Telling Friends from Foes in the Time of the Anthropocene', in Clive Hamilton, Christophe Bonneuil, and Francois Gemenne (eds), *The Anthropocene and the Global Environmental Crisis: Rethinking Modernity in a New Epoch*, pp. 145–55. London, New York: Earthscan, Routledge.

Le Roux, William, and A. White. 2004. *Voices of the San. Living in Southern Africa Today*. Cape Town: Kwela Books.

Legal Assistance Centre. 2006. *Our Land They Took. San Land Rights under Threat in Namibia*. Windhoek: Legal Assistance Centre.

Leopold, Aldo. 1949. 'The Land Ethic', in *A Sand County Almanac. With Essays on Conservation from Round River*, pp. 237–64. New York: Oxford University Press.

————. 1979. 'Some Fundamentals of Conservation in the Southwest (Edited from Typescript, 1923)', *Environmental Ethics*, 1: 131–41.

Lewis, Bridget. 2012a. 'Environmental Rights or a Right to the Environment? Exploring the Nexus Between Human Rights and Environmental Protection', *Macquarie Journal of International and Comparative Environmental Law*, 8(1): 36–47.

————. 2012b. 'Human Rights and Environmental Wrongs: Achieving Environmental Justice through Human Rights Law', *International Journal for Crime and Justice*, 1(1): 65–73.

Lombrog, Bjorn. 1998. *The Skeptical Environmentalist*. Cambridge: Cambridge University Press.

Lu Holt, Flora. 2005. 'The Catch-22 of Conservation: Indigenous Peoples, Biologists, and Cultural Change', *Human Ecology*, 33(2): 199–215.

MacCormick, Neil. 1976. 'Children's Rights: A Test-Case for Theories of Right', *Archiv Für Rechts- Und Sozialphilosophie*, 52(3): 305–17.

MacKenzie, John M. 1988. *The Empire of Nature: Hunting, Conservation and British Imperialism*. Manchester, New York: Manchester University Press.

Maffi, Luisa. 2005. 'Linguistic, Cultural, and Biological Diversity', *Annual Review of Anthropology*, 34: 599–617.

Maffi, Luisa. 2007. 'Biocultural Diversity and Sustainability', in Jules Pretty, Andrew S. Ball, Ted Benton, Julia S. Guivant, David R. Lee, David Orr, Max J. Pfeffer, and Hugh Ward (eds), *The SAGE Handbook of Environment and Society*, pp. 267–77. London: SAGE Publications Ltd.

————. 2014. 'Biocultural Approaches to Conservation and Development', in Luisa Maffi and Dilts Ortixia (eds), *Biocultural Diversity Toolkit*. Terralingua. Available at http://terralingua.org/our-work/bcd-conservation/biocultural-diversity-toolkit/ (accessed 3 January 2018).

Maffi, Luisa, and Ellen Woodley. 2010. *Biocultural Diversity Conservation: A Global Sourcebook*. London, Washington, DC: Earthscan.

Mallarach, Josep-Maria (ed.). 2012. Spiritual Values of Protected Areas of Europe: Workshop Proceedings of the International Academy for Nature Conservation on the Isle of Vilm, Germany, 2–6 November 2011. Bonn: German Federal Agency for Nature Conservation.

Mallarach, Josep-Maria, and Thymio Papayannis. 2010. 'Sacred Natural Sites in Technologically Developed Countries: Reflections from the Experience of the Delos Initiative', in Bas Verschureen, Robert Wild, Jeffrey A. McNeely, and Gonzalo Oviedo (eds), *Sacred Natural Sites. Conserving Nature & Culture*, pp. 198–208. London, Washington, DC: Earthscan.

Manus, Peter M. 2005. 'Sovereignty, Self-Determination, and Environment-Based Cultures: The Emerging Voice of Indigenous Peoples in International Law', *Wisconsin International Law Journal*, 23(4): 553–642.

Marshall, Shelley, and Samantha Balaton-Chrimes. 2016. *Tribal Claims Against the Vedanta Bauxite Mine in Niyamgiri, India: What Role Did the UK OECD National Contact Point Play in Instigating Free, Prior and Informed Consent?*, Non-Judicial Redress Mechanisms Report Series 9. Available at https://ssrn.com/abstract=2878211 (accessed 3 January 2018).

Martin, Paul S. 1966. 'Africa and Pleistocene Overkill', *Nature*, 212: 339–42.

Masolo, D.A. 2004. 'Western and African Communitarianism: A Comparison', in Kwasi Wiredu (ed.), *A Companion to African Philosophy*, pp. 483–98. Oxford: Blackwell Publishing Ltd.

May, James R., and Erin Daly. 2011. 'New Directions in Earth Rights, Environmental Rights and Human Rights: Six Facets of Constitutionally Embedded Environmental Rights Worldwide', *IUCN Academy of Environmental Law E-Journal*, Widener Law School Legal Studies Research Paper No. 11–09.

Meine, Curt. 2010. 'Conservation Biology: Past and Present', in Navjot S. Sodhi and Paul R. Ehrlich (eds), *Conservation Biology for All*, pp. 7–26. Oxford: Oxford University Press.

Mgbeoji, Ikechi. 2006. *Global Biopiracy: Patents, Plants and Indigenous Knowledge*. Vancouver, BC: UBC Press.

Millennium Ecosystem Assessment. 2005. *Ecosystem and Human Well-Being: Synthesis*. Washington, DC: Island Press.

Moller, Kai. 2012. *The Global Model of Constitutional Rights*. Oxford: Oxford University Press.

Morel, Cynthia. 2010. 'Conservation and Indigenous Peoples' Rights: Must One Necessarily Come at the Expense of the Other?', *Policy Matters*, 17: 174–80.

Morgera, Elisa. 2016. 'The Need for an International Legal Concept of Fair and Equitable Benefit-Sharing', *The European Journal of International Law*, 27(2): 353–83.

Morgera, E., E. Tsioumani, and M. Buck (eds). 2014. *Unraveling the Nagoya Protocol—A Commentary on Access and Benefit-sharing to the Convention on Biological Diversity*. Leiden, Boston: Brill.

Mutz, Kathryn M., Gary C. Bryner, and Douglas S. Kenney (eds). 2002. *Justice and Natural Resources: Concepts, Strategies, and Applications*. Washington, DC: Island Press.

Naess, Arne, '"The Deep Ecology Movement": Some Philosophical Aspects', in Environmental Philosophy, Second Edition, Michael Zimmermann et al (eds), Prentice-Hall Inc., Englewood Cliffs, NJ, 1998; reproduced in Light, Andrew, and III Rolston Holmes (eds). *Environmental Ethics: An Antology*. Malden, Oxford, Victoria: Blackwell Publishing, 2003.

Nagengast, Carole. 1997. 'Women, Minorities and Indigenous People: Universalism and Cultural Relativity', *Journal of Anthropological Research*, 53(3): 349–69.

Niezen, Ronal. 2003. *The Origins of Indigenism. Human Rights and the Politics of Identity*. Berkeley, CA: University of California Press.

Nonini, Donald M. (ed.). 2007. *The Global Idea of 'the Commons'. Critical Inventions: A Forum for Social Analysis*. New York: Berghahn Books.

Norton, Bryan G. 1984. 'Environmental Ethics and Weak Anthropocentrism', *Environmental Ethics*, 6: 131–48.

———. 1989. 'The Cultural Approach to Conservation Biology', in David Western and Mary Pearl (eds), *Conservation for the Twenty-First Century*, pp. 241–6. Oxford: Oxford University Press.

O'Neill, John. 1992. 'The Varieties of Intrinsic Value', *The Monist*, 75(2): 119–37.

O'Neill, Onora. 2004. 'Women's Rights: Whose Obligations?' in Onora O'Neill (ed.), *Bounds of Justice*, pp. 97–111. Cambridge: Cambridge University Press.

Okin, Susan Moller. 1999. 'Is Multiculturalism Bad for Women?', in Joshua Cohen, Matthew Howard, and Martha C. Nussbaum (eds), *Is Multiculturalism Bad for Women?*, pp. 7–26. Princeton: Princeton University Press.

———. 2002. '"Mistresses of Their Own Destiny": Group Rights, Gender, and Realistic Rights of Exit', *Ethics*, 112(2): 205–30.

Olson, Mancur. 1965. *The Logic of Collective Action: Public Goods and the Theory of Groups*. Cambridge, MA: Harvard University Press.

Ostrom, Elionor. 1990. *Governing the Commons. The Evolution of Institutions for Collective Action*. Cambridge: Cambridge University Press.

Oudenhoven, Friederik, Dunja Mijatovic, and Pablo Eyzaguirre. 2010. 'Bridging Managed and Natural Landscapes: The Role of Traditional (Agri)culture in Maintaining the Diversity and Resilience of Social-Ecological Systems', in C. Bèlair, K. Ichikawa, B.Y.L. Wong, and K.J. Mulongoy (eds), *Sustainable Use of Biological Diversity in Socio-Ecological Landscapes: Background to the Sotoyama Initiative*, pp. 8–21. Montreal: Secretariat of CBD.

Park, Chris C. 2001. *The Environment: Principles and Applications*. London, New York: Routledge.

Passmore, John. 1974. *Men's Responsibility for Nature: Ecological Problems and Western Traditions*. New York: Scribner.

Pearce, Fred. 2015. 'Global Extinction Rates: Why Do Estimates Vary So Wildly', *Yale Environment*, 360.

Pievani, Telmo. 2002. *Homo Sapiens e Altre Catastrofi: Per Un'archeologia Della Globalizzazione* (*Homo Sapiens and other Disasters: An Archaeology of Globalization*). Roma: Meltemi.

Pires de Carvalho, Nuno. 2007. 'From the Shaman's Hut to the Patent Office: A Road under Construction', in Charles McManis (ed.), *Biodiversity and the Law: Intellectual Property, Biotechnology & Traditional Knowledge*, pp. 241–79. London: Earthscan.

Pogge, Thomas. 2008. 'How Should Human Rights Be Conceived?', in Thomas Pogge (ed.), *World Poverty and Human Rights*, pp. 58–76. Bodmin, UK: Polity Press.

Posey, Darrell Addison. 1990. 'Intellectual Property Rights and Just Compensation for Indigenous Knowledge', *Anthropology Today*, 6(4): 13–16.

———. 1995. 'Indigenous Peoples and Traditional Resource Rights: A Basis for Equitable Relationships?', in *Workshop on Indigenous Peoples and Traditional Resource Rights*. Oxford: The Green College Centre for Environmental Policy & Understanding.

————. (ed.). 1996. *Traditional Resource Rights: International Instruments for Protection and Compensation for Indigenous Peoples and Local Communities*. Gland and Cambridge: IUCN.

————. 1998. 'Biodiversity, Genetic Resources, and Indigenous Peoples in Amazonia: (Re) Discovering the Wealth of Traditional Resources of Native Amazonians', in *AMAZONIA 2000: Development, Environment, and Geopolitics*. London: Institute of Latin American Studies University of London.

———— (ed.). 1999a. *Cultural and Spiritual Values of Biodiversity: A Complementary Contribution to the Global Biodiversity Assessment*. Nairobi: Intermediate Technology Publication.

————. 1999b. 'Introduction: Culture and Nature: The Inextricable Link', in Darrell Addison Posey (ed.), *Cultural and Spiritual Values of Biodiversity: A Complementary Contribution to the Global Biodiversity Assessment*, pp. 1–20. Nairobi: Intermediate Technology Publication.

————. 2002. 'Commodification of the Sacred through Intellectual Property Rights', *Journal of Ethnopharmacology*, 83(1–2): 3–12.

Posey, Darrell Addison, and Graham Dutfield. 1996. *Beyond Intellectual Property: Toward Traditional Resource Rights for Indigenous Peoples and Local Communities*. Ottawa, Canada: International Development Research Centre.

Pulido, Carlos Bernal. 2006. 'The Rationality of Balancing', *Archiv Für Rechts- Und Sozialphilosophie*, 92(2): 195–208.

Rajan, S. Ravi. 2011. 'Classical Environmentalism and Environmental Human Rights: An Exploration of Their Ontological Origins and Differences', *Journal of Human Rights and the Environment*, 2(1): 106–21.

Raz, Joseph. 1988. *The Morality of Freedom*. Oxford: Clarendon Press.

————. 2010. 'Human Rights without Foundations', in Samantha Besson and John Tasioulas (eds), *The Philosophy of International Law*, pp. 321–37. Oxford: Oxford University Press.

Redford, Kent. 1991. 'The Ecologically Noble Savage', *Cultural Survival Quarterly*, 15(1): 46–8.

Reed, James, Josh van Vianen, Elizabeth L. Deakin, Jos Barlow, and Terry Sunderland. 2016. 'Integrated Landscape Approaches to Managing Social and Environmental Issues in the Tropics: Learning from the Past to Guide the Future', *Global Change Biology*, 22(7): 2540–54.

Reed, Mark S. 2008. 'Stakeholder Participation for Environmental Man- agement: A Literature Review', *Biological Conservation*, 141(10): 2417–31.

Reeves, Hubert, Joël de Rosnay, Yves Coppens, and Dominique Simonnet. 1996. *La plus Belle Histoire Du Monde. Les Secrets de Nos Origines (The*

Most Beautiful History of the World: The Secrets of Our Origins). Paris: Editions du Seuil.

Regan, Tom. 1985. 'The Case for Animal Rights', in Peter Singer (ed.), *In Defense of Animals*, pp. 13–26. Oxford: Basil Blackwell.

————. 2012. 'Animal Rights: What's in a Name', in Andrew Light and Holmes Rolston (eds), *Environmental Ethics: An Anthology*, pp. 65–71. Malden, Oxford, Victoria: Blackwell Publishing.

Richardson, Benjamin J. 2008. 'The Ties That Bind: Indigenous Peoples and Environmental Governance', *Comparative Research in Law & Political Economy*, 4(5).

Roe, Dilys, Gonzalo Oviedo, Luis Pabon, Michael Painter, Kent Redford, Linda Siegele, Jenny Springer, and Kristen Walker Painemilla. 2010. 'Conservation and Human Rights: The Need for International Standards', *IIED Briefing*, no. May.

Routley, Richard, and Val Routley. 1980. 'Human Chauvinism and Environmental Ethics', in C. Mannison, M.A. McRobbie, and Richard Sylvan (Routley), *Environmental Philosophy*, pp. 121–23. Canberra: Australian National University.

Ruppel, Oliver C. 2008. 'Third-Generation Human Rights and the Protection of the Environment in Namibia', in Nico Horn and Anton Bosl (eds), *Human Rights and the Rule of Law in Namibia*, pp. 101–20. Windhoek: Macmillan Namibia.

Sajeva, Giulia. 2015. 'Rights with Limits: Biocultural Rights—Between Self-Determination and Conservation of the Environment', *Journal of Human Rights and the Environment*, 6(1): 30–54.

Sajeva, Giulia. 2017. 'Human Rights and the Environment: A Hard Balance to Strike', *Ragion Pratica*, no. 2: 525–52.

Sanderson, Steven E., and Kent H. Redford. 2003. 'Contested Relationships between Biodiversity Conservation and Poverty Alleviation', *Oryx*, 37(4): 389–90.

Sands, Philippe, Jacqueline Peel, Adriana Fabra, and Ruth MacKenzie. 2012. *Principles of International Environmental Law*. Cambridge: Cambridge University Press.

Savaresi, Annalisa. 2012. 'The Human Rights Dimension of REDD', *Review of European, Comparative and International Environmental Law*, 21(2): 102–13.

Schmidt, Paige M., and Markus J. Peterson. 2009. 'Biodiversity Conservation and Indigenous Land Management in the Era of Self-Determination', *Conservation Biology*, 23 (6): 1458–66.

Secretariat of CBD. 2004. *The Ecosystem Approach (CBD Guidelines)*. Montreal: Secretariat of CBD.

Sheehan, Linda, and Grant Wilson. 2015. 'Fighting for Our Shared Future: Protecting Both Human Rights and Nature's Rights', a report by the Earth Law Center. Available at http://static1.squarespace. com/static/55914fd1e4b01fb0b851a814/t/5666020169a91a17ec 7be3d1/1449525761543/Fighting+for+Our+Shared+Future+-+ Earth+Law+Center+(Full+Page+Read)+-+Updated.pdf (accessed 3 January 2018).

Shiel, Matthew Phipps. 1901. *The Purple Cloud*. London: Chatto & Windus.

Shrumm, Holly, and Harry Jonas. 2012. *Biocultural Community Protocols: A Toolkit for Community Facilitators. Integrated Participatory and Legal Empowerment Tools to Support Communities to Secure Their Rights, Responsibilities, Territories, and Areas.* Cape Town: Natural Justice.

Singer, Peter. 1975. *Animal Liberation*. New York: Harper Collins Publishers.

Slikkerveer, Jan L. 1999. 'Ethnoscience, "TEK" and Its Application to Conservation', in Darrell Addison Posey (ed.), *Cultural and Spiritual Values of Biodiversity: A Complementary Contribution to the Global Biodiversity Assessment*, pp. 169–258. Nairobi: Intermediate Technology Publication.

Sobrevila, Claudia. 2008. *The Role of Indigenous Peoples in Biodiversity Conservation: The Natural but Often Forgotten Partners.* Washington, DC: The International Bank for Reconstruction and Development.

Society for Conservation Biology. Available online at https://conbio.org/ publications/science/ (last accessed on 17 February 2017).

Stevens, Stan (ed.) 2014. *Indigenous Peoples, National Parks, and Protected Areas: A New Paradigm Linking Conservation, Culture, and Rights.* Tucson: The University of Arizona Press.

Stone, Christopher. 1988. 'Moral Pluralism and the Course of Environmental Ethics', *Environmental Ethics*, 10: 139–54.

Stork, Nigel E. 2010. 'Re-Assessing Current Extinction Rates', *Biodiversity and Conservation*, 19(2): 357–71.

Subcommission on Quaternary Stratigraphy. 2016. 'Working Group on the Anthropocene', Available online at https://quaternary.stratigraphy.org/ workinggroups/anthropocene/

Suzuki, David. 1999. 'Finding a New Story', in Darrell Addison Posey (ed.), *Cultural and Spiritual Values of Biodiversity: A Complementary Contribution to the Global Biodiversity Assessment*, pp. 72–3. Nairobi: Intermediate Technology Publication.

Swiderska, Krystyna, Alejandro Argumedo, Yiching Song, Jingsong Li, Ruchi Pant, Herclio Herrera, Doris Mutta, Peter Munyi, and S. Vedavathy. 2009. *Protecting Community Rights over Traditional Knowledge. Implications of Customary Laws and Practices. Key Findings and Recommendations*

2005–2009. International Institute for Environment and Development. Available at http://pubs.iied.org/14591IIED/ (accessed 3 January 2018).

Sylvain, Renée. 2002. '"Land, Water, and Truth": San Identity and Global Indigenism', *American Anthropologist*, 104(4): 1074–1085.

———. 2011. 'At the Intersections: San Women and the Rights of Indigenous Peoples in Africa', *The International Journal of Human Rights*, 15(1): 89–110.

Sylvan (Routley), Richard. 1973. 'Is There a Need for a New, Environmental, Ethic?' in *Philosophy and Science: Morality and Culture: Technology and Man*, Proceedings of the XV World Congress of Philosophy, Varna, Bulgaria. Sofia.

Taylor, Julie. 2005. 'Land, Resources and Visibility: The Origins and Implications of Land Mapping in Namibia's West Caprivi', PhD Thesis, University of Oxford, Oxford.

Taylor, Paul W. 1986. *Respect for Nature: A Theory of Environmental Ethics*. Princeton: Princeton University Press.

Taylor, Prue. 1998. 'From Environmental to Ecological Human Rights: A New Dynamic in International Law?', *The Georgetown International Environmental Law Review*, 10(2): 309–97.

———. 2008. 'Ecological Integrity and Human Rights: Introducing the Rights versus Responsibilities Debate', in Laura Westra, Klaus Bosselmann, and Richard Westra (eds), *Reconciling Human Existence with Ecological Integrity*, 89–108. London, Sterling, VA: Earthscan.

Ten Kate, Kerry, and Sarah A. Laird. 1999. *The Commercial Use of Biodiversity: Access to Genetic Resources and Benefit Sharing*. Kent, UK: Earthscan Publications Ltd.

Terborgh, John. 2000. 'The Fate of Tropical Forests: A Matter of Stewardship', *Conservation Biology*, 14(5): 1358–61.

Tobin, Brendan. 2009. 'Setting Protection of TK to Rights: Placing Human Rights and Customary Law at the Heart of TK Governance', in C. Evanson Kamau and Gerd Winter (eds), *Genetic Resources, Traditional Knowledge & the Law*, pp. 101–118. Sterling: Earthscan Publication Ltd.

Tsosie, Rebecca. 1996. 'Tribal Environmental Policy in an Era of Self-Determination: The Role of Ethics, Economics, and Traditional Ecological Knowledge', *Vermont Law Review*, 21: 225–333.

UN. 1986. 'Study of the Problem of Discrimination against Indigenous Populations', E/CN.4/RES/1986/35. Geneva: United Nations Commission on Human Rights.

———. 2004. *Report of the Third Session of UN Permanent Forum on Indigenous Issues, 10–21 May 2004*. New York: United Nations Permanent Forum on Indigenous Issue.

————. 2009. *State of the World's Indigenous Peoples*. New York: United Nations Department of Economic and Social Affairs.

UNEP. 2011. *Report of the Expert Group Meeting of Local Community Representatives Within the Context of Article 8j and Related Provisions of the Convention on Biological Diversity*, Vol. UNEP/CBD/WG8J/7/8/Add.1. Montreal: UNEP.

UNGA. 2016. *Report of the Special Rapporteur of the Human Rights Council on the Rights of Indigenous Peoples, Victoria Tauli-Corpuz*, Vol. A/71/229. Available at http://unsr.vtaulicorpuz.org/site/images/docs/annual/2016-annual-ga-a-71-229-en.pdf (accessed 3 January 2018).

Valderrama, Guillen Calvo, and Salvatore Arico. 2010. 'Traditional Knowledge: From Environmental Management to Territorial Development', in Suneetha M. Subramanian and Balakrishna Pisupati (eds), *Traditional Knowledge in Policy and Practice*, pp. 208–25. Hong Kong: United Nations University.

Varner, Gary E. 1995. 'Can Animal Rights Activists Be Environmentalists', in Don E. Marietta and Lester Embree (eds), *Environmental Philosophy and Environmental Activism*, pp. 169–202. Lanham, MD: Rowman & Littlefield Publishers.

Verschuuren, Bas, Robert Wild, Jeffery A. McNeely, and Gonzalo Oviedo (eds). 2010. *Sacred Natural Sites: Conserving Nature & Culture*. London, Washington, DC: Earthscan.

Waldron, Jeremy. 1984. 'Introduction', in Jeremy Waldron (ed.), *Theories of Rights*, pp. 1–20. Oxford: Oxford University Press.

————. 1993. 'The Right to Do Wrong', in Jeremy Waldron (ed.), *Liberal Rights: Collected Papers, 1981–1991*, pp. 63–87. Cambridge: Cambridge University Press.

Walker, Beth (ed.). 2012. *State of the World's Minorities and Indigenous Peoples 2012*. London: Minority Rights Group International.

Wenar, Leif. 2011. 'Rights', in Edward N. Zalta (ed.), *The Stanford Encyclopaedia of Philosophy*. Available at https://plato.stanford.edu/entries/rights/ (accessed 3 January 2018).

White, Lynn. 1967. 'The Historical Roots of Our Ecological Crisis', *Science*, 155(3767): 1203–7.

Wild, Robert. 2010. 'Nature Saint and Holy Island, Ancient Values in a Modern Economy: The Enduring Influence of St Cuthbert and Lindisfarne, United Kingdom', in Bas Verschuuren, Robert Wild, Jeffrey A. McNeely, and Gonzalo Oviedo (eds), *Sacred Natural Sites: Conserving Nature & Culture*, pp. 77–97. London, Washington, DC: Earthscan.

Wilshusen, Peter R., Steven R. Brechin, Crystal L. Fortwangler, and Patrick C. West. 2002. 'Reinventing a Square Wheel: Critique of a Resurgent

"Protection Paradigm" in International Biodiversity Conservation', *Society & Natural Resources*, 15: 17–40.

Wilson, Edward O. 2001. *The Diversity of Life*. London: Penguin Books.

Wilson, Ken. 2016. 'Flourishing at Twenty: On Context and Foundations in the Rise of the Concept of Biocultural Diversity', *Terralingua Langscape*, 5(2): 10–15.

World Commission on Environment and Development. 1987. *Our Common Future*. Oxford: Oxford University Press.

World Resources Institute. 2005. *The Wealth of the Poor: Managing Ecosystems to Fight Poverty*. Washington, DC: World Resources Institute.

Xanthaki, Alexandra. 2007. *Indigenous Rights and United Nations Standards: Self-Determination, Culture and Land*. Cambridge: Cambridge University Press.

Zalasiewicz, Jan, Colin Waters, and Martin J. Head. 2017. 'Anthropocene: Its Stratigraphic Basis', *Nature*, 541: 289.

Ziegler, Jean, Grégoire de Kalbermatten, Liliane Ortega, Christophe Golay, Claire Mahon, Sally-Anne Way, and Michaela Büschi. 2008. 'Human Rights and Desertification. Exploring the Complementarity of International Human Rights Law and the United Nations Convention to Combat Desertification', Issue paper 1, Secretariat of the United Nations Convention to Combat Desertification, Bonn. Available at http://www.ohchr.org/Documents/Issues/ClimateChange/Submissions/UNCCD.pdf (accessed 3 January 2018).

Zimmerman, Michael J. 2015. 'Intrinsic vs. Extrinsic Value', in Edward N. Zalta (ed.), *The Stanford Encyclopaedia of Philosophy*. Available at https://plato.stanford.edu/entries/value-intrinsic-extrinsic/ (accessed 3 January 2018).

Index

Aarhus Convention (2001), 54n16
access and benefit sharing (ABS), 83, 108n46
access to land, rights regarding, 127
aesthetic value, notion of, 13
African Charter, 50n1, 86n19, 87
African Commission on Human and People's Rights, 57n22, 86–7
African Court on Human and Peoples' Rights, 57n22, 124
African Union (AU), 87
Agenda 21, 82, 102n42
Agreement for the Implementation of the UN Convention on the Law of the Sea (1995), 46
American Revolution, 24, 25, 31
ancestral land occupancy, 128
animal interests, 15–17
animal rights, 148; and interests, 15–17; recognition of, 15
Anthropocene, 6; human rights in, 146–9

anthropocentric ethics, 8–12, 103, 143, 148
Article 8j of the CBD, 45, 82, 122

balancing, of human rights, 27–8, 129n10, 141
Bavikatte, Sanjay Kabir, xvii, 26, 77, 83, 101, 114, 118, 122, 127
benefit sharing, right to, 98, 127; see also access and benefit sharing (ABS)
Bennet, Tom, 113, 118, 150
biocentric ethics, 15, 17–18
biocultural community protocol (BCP), 130, 136
biocultural diversity, 150; and conservation, 64–71
biocultural rights, xviii, 122, 141; and challenges to imposing duties, 118–21; concept of, xvii, 20, 21–2, 37, 77, 101, 116,

128, 146; court cases and laws regarding, 86–94; as emerging rights, 26, 80–95; foundations of, xxi, 128; as human rights, 31, 148; international documents, conventions, and declarations, 81–6; intrinsic characteristic of, 149; landscape approach to, 126, 145; meaning of, 76–80; recognition of, 124, 128
biodiversity conservation, 64, 126
biodiversity loss, 5, 127n9
biological diversity, 59, 66, 66n38, 71, 101, 112
biopiracy, 68n41, 98
biotic community, 17–19
Bobbio, Norberto, 24
Bolivian Constitution, 58n23, 103n43
Brundtland report, *Our Common Future* (1987), 12–13, 81
Bushmen, 131
Bwabwata National Park: Khwe people of, 129, 130–5, 145; management of, 135; poaching in, 135; wildlife management, 135

Cancun Agreement (2009), 86
Caprivi Game Park, 132
Caprivi Strip, 130
carbon emissions, 85, 127
carbon stocks, terrestrial, 85
cattle keeping, 138, 140
claimant, 23, 56, 111–12, 120n5, 139
clean water, right to, 55

climate change, 1, 6, 85, 105, 118, 127n9
Cobo, Martínez, 38
collective rights, 36, 40
colonialism, 59
colonial science, 61
common property, 63, 106
communal lands, utilization of, 134n15
community-based conservation, 64, 128
community-based organizations, 111, 120
Conference of the Parties, 46, 85
conservation area, creation of, 87
conservation biology, 59n25
Conservation International, 70
conservation of the environment, xix, 7, 20, 22, 31, 46, 51, 53, 56, 70, 76, 78, 80; anthropocentric approaches to, 10; jurisprudence on issues related to, 94; role of indigenous peoples and local communities in, 83, 95; value of, 87; of wilderness, 61
conservation projects: community-based, 64; rights-based, 64
conservation refugees, 62
conservation science *see* conservation biology
constitutional democracies, 25
Convention 169 on Indigenous and Tribal Peoples, 39n24, 41
Convention on Biological Diversity (CBD), xviii, 45, 77; Article 2 of, 5n9; Article 8j of, 45, 82, 122; Article 10c of, 82; Conference of the Parties, 46; ecosystem

approach' proposed by, 127n9;
Nagoya Protocol (2010), 45–6,
77, 102n42, 123
Conventions on Elimination of all
Forms of Discrimination against
Women (1979), 32
Conventions on Rights of Persons
with Disabilities (2007), 32
Conventions on Rights of the Child
(1989), 32
Conventions Relating to the Status
of Refugees (1951), 32
Convention to Combat
Desertification (1994), 46
court cases and laws, regarding
biocultural rights, 86–94
Crawfurd, John, 72
Crutzen, Paul, 6
cultivation of land, impact of
wildlife on, 133
cultural diversity, 37, 64, 91, 98–9,
127, 138
cultural identity: conservation of,
100, 110–12, 116; development
of, 112; promotion of, 100, 110;
protection of, 113; rights to,
107–8, 143
cultural rights, 128
custodianship, 20
customary laws, xviii, 69

deep ecology, concept of, 10
Devil's Claw, 135n17
discrimination, 37, 45, 107; racial,
43
domesticated species, 5
Dongaria Kondh tribe (India),
89–90

double foundation, 99–104
Dutfield, Graham, 96
duty-based, 117
duty holders, xxi, 110–14

Earth Summit see Rio Declaration
(1992)
ecocentric ethics, 18–20, 148
ecocide, 4
ecological limitations, 148
ecology, meaning of, 10n15
ecosystem approach, 127n9
ecosystem services, 67
ecovillage, 151n2
Ecuadorian Constitution of 2008,
57n23
Endorois (indigenous people of
Africa), 87–8
Endorois Welfare Council v. *Kenya*,
xviii, 86–7
environment: exploitation of, 60;
and human right, 50–64; for
rights, 50–3; rights for, 53–7;
value of, 8
environmental activism, 54
environmental allies, 64–75
environmental conservation, 22, 128,
130, 142, 148; anthropocentric
approaches to, 10–14; biocultural
diversity and, 64–71; meaning
of, 17; non-anthropocentric
approaches to, 14–20; as prerequisite for the well-being, 8; Western
approaches towards, 9, 14
environmental crisis, 2, 53, 75,
121; and destruction caused by
humans, 5; meaning of, 1n2;
value, matter of, 7–10

environmental damage, 119; detrimental effect on human rights, 56n22;
environmental degradation, 52, 56, 152
environmental ethics, 8, 14; anthropocentric, 8–9, 11–12; biocentric, 15, 17–18; ecocentric, 18–20; non-anthropocentric, 8–9, 148; Western, 9, 11
environmental fascism, 17–18, 148
environmental hazards, 51
environmental law, 55, 77, 119, 152; Environmental Protection Act (1986), India, 90; Forest Conservation Act (1980), India, 90; Scheduled Tribes and Other Forest Dwellers (Recognition of Forest Rights) Act (2006), India, 90–1; Te Awa Tupua (Whanganui River Claims Settlement) Act (2017), New Zealand, 92–4
environmental protection, 11, 50, 147; balance with human rights, 149; see also environmental conservation
Environmental Protection Act (1986), India, 90
environmental rights, 54, 147; development of, 53; effectiveness of, 56; enforcement of, 56; procedural, 53–4, 56
environmental stewardship, 105, 108, 125
environmental sustainability, 47
ethnic minorities, 37

Ethnological Society of London, 72
ethno-nationalism, 41
European Court of Human Rights, 57n22, 124
exotic diseases, 7
expression, freedom of, 29–30
extinction of species, 2; because of human beings, 3; Big Five mass extinctions, 5, 7; methods and models for calculation of, 6; Pleistocene extinction, 5; rates of, 5; sixth mass extinction, 5, 7

family life, right to, 52–3, 57n22
farmers' rights, 84
Feinberg, Joel, 15
'fences-and-fines' approaches, to conservation, 143
Food and Agriculture Organization (FAO), 84
Food and Agriculture Organization International Treaty on Plant Genetic Resources for Food and Agriculture (2001), 46
food plants, 135, 138
food, right to, 129n10
food security, 52, 127n9
Forest Conservation Act (1980), India, 90
forest-dependent communities, 86
fortress conservation, 64, 74, 78, 121; at expense of indigenous peoples, 62; in Yellowstone National Park, 61n30, 62
foundations of rights, xxi, 30–1, 57, 128
French Revolution, 24, 25, 31

fundamental rights, violation of, 13, 24, 51, 52, 65

game theory, 63n34
general interest, xx, 27–31, 57, 112, 116–17, 120, 123, 143, 147, 150
genetic resources: conservation of, 151; intellectual property rights over, 151; plant genetic diversity, 84; principle of sovereignty of states over, 83
global biodiversity, 5
Global Ecovillage Network, 151n2
gram sabhas (village assemblies), 90–1
greening, of human rights, 53, 56, 57n22
green technologies, 78
group rights, xviii, xx, 32–8, 79, 88, 100–1

habitat, 2, 6–7, 10n15, 57, 69, 73n45
hapu tribe, 93
Hardin, Garrett, 62
Hartney, Michael, 35n16
health practices, right to, 44
healthy environment, right to live in, 55
Hingston, Richard, 61n29
Holocene, 4, 6
Homo sapiens, 1; characteristics of, 4; ecological roles of, 3
human interests, protection of, 56
humankind, 34, 102–3, 110, 114, 116, 120, 143–4, 149

human population, 23, 63; growth of, 4, 6
human psychology, 20, 149
human rights, xviii, 20; abolishing differences between citizens and non-citizens, 31; in Anthropocene, 146–9; beyond the individual, 31–8; biocultural rights as, 31, 148; code of duties, 25; defined, 21–4; emergence of, 24; and environment, 50–64; ethics of, 148; evolution of, 34; expression, freedom of, 29–30; functioning and limits of, 27–31; goals of, 27; greening of, 53, 56, 57n22; group rights, 32–8; harmonization of, 55; holistic perspective of, 25; interest theory of, 22; of local communities, 45–9, 149; moral, political and legal, 24–6; moral right, 26; movement, freedom of, 30; protection of, 53; and protection of the environment, 149; sui generis, 115–21; trump and balance, 27–8; UN Commission on Human Rights, 39; universality and specialization of, 31–2; universality of, 32–3; UN Universal Declaration on Human Rights, 26; vis-à-vis general interest, 29–31
hunter-gatherers, 131
hunting practices: ban on, 133; of colonizers, 60n28; evolution of, 60n28

Indian Ministry of Environment and Forest (MoEF), 88
indigenous peoples, xvii, xviii, 113; biocultural rights of, 123, 145; of Bwabwata National Park, xxii; colonial and postcolonial history of, 120; concerns for ecological integrity, 117; difference with local communities, 121–5; Endorois people of Africa, 87; as environmental allies, 64–75; environmental rights of, 126; fortress conservation approaches, 62; human rights of, xxi, 2, 21, 38–45, 128, 144, 149; hunter-gatherers, 131; Khwe people, 145; legal position of, 124; lifestyles and practices of, 144; marginalization of, 124; non-discrimination, right to, 43; property systems of, 65; removal or decimation of, 62; rights to welfare and development, 44; right to self-determination of, 41, 116, 124; role in protection of the environment, 121; stewardship role of, 143; UN Declaration on the Rights of Indigenous Peoples, 26
Indigenous Peoples and Local Communities' Conserved Territories and Areas (ICCAs), 69
individual rights, 34–7, 57
Industrial Revolution, 5
instrumental value, 9–10, 57, 99
Integrated Rural Development and Nature Conservation (IRDNC), 135, 136, 140

intellectual property rights, 91, 151
Inter-American Court of Human Rights, 48, 48n47, 55n22, 122, 124
interest, and animal rights, 15–17
interest theory of rights, 15, 22
International Commission on Stratigraphy, 6
International Convention on the Elimination of All Forms of Racial Discrimination, 43
International Covenant on Civil and Political Rights (1966), 32
International Covenant on Economic, Social and Cultural Rights (1966), 32
International Institute for Environment and Development, 67
International Labour Organization (ILO), 39; Convention 169 on Indigenous and Tribal Peoples, 41
International Treaty on Plant Genetic Resources for Food and Agriculture (ITPGRFA), 84
International Tropical Timber Agreement (2006), 46
International Union for Conservation of Nature and Natural Resources (IUCN), 46, 70; Programme 2017–2020, 70; Red List, 6n10, 89; World Conservation Congress, 70
intrinsic value, 9–10, 13, 16, 24, 29, 31, 34, 100, 102, 116, 148
invasive species, 2, 7, 17–18, 93, 105

Jonas, Hans, 8
justification of rights, 22n3, 32, 57, 87, 99

Kenya, 68, 87
Khwe of Bwabwata National Park, 129, 130–5, 145; biocultural rights, 139; culture and traditions of, 136–41; customary land rights, 134n15; food sources for, 133; indigenous status and rights, 139; Integrated Rural Development and Nature Conservation (IRDNC), 135, 136; Khwe Traditional Authority, 134; knowledge and practices, 136, 137; life of, 134; natural products used by, 132; transmission of traditional knowledge to new generations, 138
knowledge, value of, 13
Kutia Kondh tribe (India), 89–90
Kwando river, 132
Kyaramacan Peoples Association, 135, 135n17, 136, 140

Lake Bogoria Game Reserve, Kenya, 87
land and natural resources, rights to, 105–6
land degradation, 51
land evictions, 143
land, right to, 108n46, 109
landscape approach, 126, 127, 145
League of Nations, 130
legal rights, 22n3, 25–6, 31, 49, 115

legal systems, 33n13, 39, 73, 81n6, 103, 117–18
Leopold, Aldo, 18; Land Ethic, The (1949), 19
Lescarbot, Marc, 72
life, right to, 52, 129n10
lifespan, of a species, 3n7
limits of human rights: general interest, 29–31; trump and balance, 27–8
linguistic diversity, 66n38
local communities, xviii, 113; ancestral land of, 49; characteristics of, 46; colonial and postcolonial history of, 120; definition of, 45, 47; difference with indigenous peoples, 121–5; as environmental allies, 64–75; environmental rights of, 126; Moiwana local community, 48; property systems of, 65; proposal for environmental conservation, 149–54; rights of, 2, 45–9, 129, 149; role in protection of the environment, 121
local landscape, fragmentation of, 127

Maori tribe, 92, 94
marginalization, of indigenous peoples, 124
market economy, 73
mass extinction, 5, 7
Mbukushu (Bantu people), 132, 134
medicinal plants, 133, 135, 138
Millennium Development Goals, 51

minorities, 37, 41, 43
Moiwana local community, 48
moral right, 22, 25, 26, 80
moral standing, 148; of animals,
16–17, 19; of entities other
than human beings, 14; of the
environment, 15; of living beings,
15, 17
movement, freedom of, 30

Naess, Arne, 10
Nagoya Protocol (2010), 45–6,
77, 82, 83n14, 102n42, 123;
obligations under, 84
Namibia, 36, 130–2
national park, creation of, 61; use of
land for, 61
native lands, 105
native peoples: environmental
practices of, 121; exploitation
of, 98
naturalistic fallacy, 148
Natural Justice: Lawyers for
Communities and the
Environment, 130n11, 136
natural resources: conservation of,
11; destruction of, 67; overexploitation of, 67; rights to access,
136; sustainable management of,
81; sustainable use of, 134n15
Nature Conservancy, 70
nature's rights, idea of, 57n23
'newly discovered' lands, 64
Niezen, Ronald, 33
Niyamgiri case (India), 88–92
Niyamgiri Hills, 89
'noble savage' myth, 71–2, 113, 118,
144

nomadic people, 131
non-anthropocentric ethics, 8, 9;
adoption of, 148
non-discrimination, right to, 43
non-governmental organizations,
120, 135, 136
non-hazardous environment, right
to, 55
non-instrumental value, 10, 17
North–South divide, 59, 59n26

Okawango river, 132
Okin, Susan, 37n20
Ostrom, Elinor, 65; system of
commons, 65
Our Common Future (1987), 12, 81

Paris Agreement (2016), 85
pastoralist and agricultural practices, 151
plant genetic diversity, conservation
and development of, 84
Pleistocene extinction, 5
Pleistocene period, 3–4
poaching, 135, 138
political rights, 25, 40, 54
Posey, Darrell, xxi, 65, 95, 97–9,
102, 127
poverty alleviation, 58; challenges
of, 127n9
prior informed consent, 42, 54, 62,
83, 91, 98, 108, 111, 138, 143
pristine ecosystem, meaning of,
60n27
procedural environmental rights, 53,
54n16, 56, 108, 143
property systems: commons,
62n33, 63, 65, 77n1; of

indigenous peoples, 65; of local communities, 65; private, 65; state-controlled, 65
protected areas: establishment of, 55, 78; rights regarding, 127; wilderness in, 61
protected environment, concept of, 119

Ramsar Convention on Wetlands (1971), 46
REDD+, 85–6
Redford, Kent, 72
Reducing Emissions from Deforestation and Forest Degradation (REDD), 85
Regan, Tom, 16, 19
religions 151
responsibility: ethic of, 8; towards future generations, 13; towards the environment, xviii
right holder, 17, 22n3, 23, 29, 149, 152
rights-based conservation, 142–3
Rio Declaration (1992), 81; Agenda 21, 82; principle 22 of, 45; UN Conference on Environment and Development, 45n45
river pollution, 54
Round River Conservation Research Centre, 133
Rousseau, Jean-Jacques, 72

sacred natural sites, 69n43; protection of, 151
San people, 36, 131–2, 135n17
Saxena Committee, 90
Scheduled Tribes, 89

Scheduled Tribes and Other Forest Dwellers (Recognition of Forest Rights) Act (2006), India, 90–1
seed banks, 78
self-consciousness, notion of, 15
self-determination, right to, 35–6, 40n29, 41, 43, 65, 106–7, 143; of indigenous people, 41, 111, 116, 124
self-government rights, 151
self-identification, 39, 46
self-preservation, of ethnic community, 36
Singer, Peter, 16
Solomonic settlement, 28
South African Defence Force, 132
sovereignty of states, principle of, 29, 83
specialization, of human rights, 31–2
Special Rapporteur on Human Rights and the Environment (2015), 51, 71
special rights, 32, 34, 36, 152
species approach, guiding principle of, 127n9
species succession, 2
speech, freedom of, 55
standard of living, 44, 52–3
state lands, usage of, 151
stewards of the environment: double foundation, 99–104; duties of, 110–14; environmental stewardship, 105; rights of, 104–10
Stockholm Declaration (1972): adoption of, 51, 152n3; Principle 1 of, 55, 55n18; Principle 19 of,

152; United Nations Conference on Human Environment, 152n3

super predators, 3

Supreme Court of India, 88–90

sustainability, 47, 68, 72, 119–20, 129n10, 139, 144, 152

sustainable development: concept of, 12; Sustainable Development Goals, 51

sustainable lifestyles, 73, 79, 113, 123–5, 129, 145

sustainable livelihood, 83

Sylvan, Richard (Routley), 14

Taylor, Paul W., 17

Te Awa Tupua (Whanganui River Claims Settlement) Act (2017), New Zealand, 92–4

third-generation rights, 77

thought, freedom of, 55

timber exploitation, 61

tourism, community-based, 132

Traditional Authorities Act (2000), Namibia, 134n15

traditional authority, 134, 138, 140

traditional communities, 123, 134n15

traditional ethics, xvii, 8, 20

traditional knowledge, 64, 69, 78, 81, 83, 85, 127, 134, 137; teaching of, 107; transmission of, 140

traditional medicines, right to use, 44

traditional resource rights (TRRs), 95–9, 101–2, 127; concept of, xxi; foundational justification of, 99

tragedy of the commons, theory of, 62, 65

trophy hunting, 132, 135n17

trump, rights as, 27–8

United Nations (UN): Commission on Human Rights, 39; Conference on Human Environment, 51, 152n3; Convention on Combating Desertification (1994), 85n16; Convention on Elimination of all Forms of Discrimination against Women (1979), 32; Convention on Rights of Persons with Disabilities (2007), 32; Conventions on Rights of the Child (1989), 32; Convention on Status of Refugees (1951), 32; Declaration on Rights of Indigenous Peoples (UNDRIP), 39, 43–5, 95; Declaration on Rights of Minorities, 43; Environmental Program and the Nature Conservancy, 70; Framework Convention on Climate Change (UNFCCC), 85; General Assembly (UNGA), 39m, 50, 71; High Commissioner for Human Rights (UNHCHR), 51; International Covenant on Civil and Political Rights (1966), 32; International Covenant on Economic, Social and Cultural Rights (1966), 32; Universal Declaration of Human Rights

(1948), 26, 28, 32, 43; World
Commission on Environment
and Development, 12, 81
Universal Declaration of Human
Rights (1948), 26, 32, 43; Article
29 of, 28
universality, 31, 32
unsustainable practices, 128
utilitarian, 13, 16

value of environment: aesthetic,
13; instrumental and non-
instrumental, 10; life on Earth
and, 10; matter of, 7–10
Vedanta Resources, 89

Waitangi, Treaty of (1840), 92n37
Waitangi Tribunal, 92, 92n37
well-being, human, 10–11, 51;
components of, 12
West Caprivi Nature Park, 132
Western legal systems, 117
Whanganui iwi, 93
Whanganui River Agreement
(2012), New Zealand, 92

Whanganui River, New Zealand,
92; Te Awa Tupua (Whanganui
River Claims Settlement) Act
(2017), New Zealand, 92–4;
Whanganui iwi and hapu
(sub-tribes), 93; Whanganui
River Agreement (2012), New
Zealand, 92
wilderness: concept of, 10n14;
preservation of, 60, 61
Wi Parata judgment (1877), 92n37
women's rights, 124n8
workers' rights, 124n8
World Wide Fund for Nature
(WWF), 46, 70

Yellowstone National Park,
Montana, 61; fortress conservation in, 61n30, 62

Zambezi Region, 130, 132
Zambia, 130
Zimbabwe, 130, 131

About the Author

Giulia Sajeva is an Italian scholar who has discovered her passion for the conservation of the environment and its relationship with human rights since her MSc in Conservation Science, awarded by the Imperial College London. Her thesis on access and benefit sharing and indigenous peoples' traditional knowledge brought her to South Africa and Botswana. After an internship at the Conventions and Policies Section of the Royal Botanic Gardens, Kew—which lead her to help in the drafting ethical guidelines for botanical research with indigenous peoples and local communities—Sajeva completed a doctorate in Human Rights at the Department of Law, Università degli Studi di Palermo, Italy, where her thesis focused on biocultural rights.

Sajeva also has an MSc in Rule of Law and Constitutional Democracy by the Università degli studi di Genova, Italy. She is currently the vice president of the Religion and Conservation Biology Working Group of the Society of Conservation Biology, Washington, DC, and she also collaborates with the Università degli Studi di Palermo.